DISASTER
BY THE BAY

DISASTER BY THE BAY

THE GREAT SAN FRANCISCO EARTHQUAKE AND FIRE OF 1906

"Not in history has a modern imperial city been so completely destroyed. San Francisco is gone!"
                                        –Jack London, April 19, 1906

H. PAUL JEFFERS

THE LYONS PRESS
Guilford, Connecticut
An imprint of The Globe Pequot Press

FOR RUSS BOMBERGER

The Lyons Press is an imprint of The Globe Pequot Press.

10 9 8 7 6 5 4 3 2 1

Printed in the United States of America.

Designed by M. A. Dubé

ISBN 1-59228-139-7

Library of Congress Cataloging-in-Publication data is available on file.

Contents

Prologue

☙

GAUDY DAYS, BAWDY NIGHTS

❧

ITH A CIGAR IN ONE CORNER OF HIS fleshy lips, a flowered vest, a huge diamond ring sparkling on a pudgy middle finger, a necktie held by a stickpin with an even bigger stone, and with a greedy glint in his beady eyes, Jerome Bassity calculated that during the night of Tuesday, April 17, 1906, his Barbary Coast whorehouses had raked in sacks of money.

Even after the usual cuts to political boss Abe Ruef, Mayor Eugene Schmitz, and the top men of the police department in order to stay in operation, San Francisco's "king" of prostitution was pocketing from six to ten thousand dollars a month. Girls and women working on their backs every day and around the clock had raised him to a financial par with the nabobs and society snobs in Nob Hill mansions who had reaped their fortunes on the backs of laborers who had mined for gold and built the railroads.

Although money had not earned Bassity the respectability that wealth bestowed on the names of Stanford, Crocker, Huntington, Hopkins, Mackay, Baldwin, Fair, O'Brien, and others, they were alike in having seen and grabbed opportunities afforded by a hilly city on the northern point of a narrow thirty-mile peninsula at 37 degrees, 47 minutes north latitude separating a bay from the Pacific Ocean. But the first white men to venture onto the peninsula that became San Francisco had arrived by land. Under the command of Don Gaspar de Portola, Spaniards discovered the bay in November 1769. When a settlement was established seven years later, a presidio (fortress) was built. Called Yerba Buena, the village included a mission that its founder, Father Junipero Serra, named San Francisco de Asis.

The region was in Spanish and then Mexican hands until 1846, when the United States Marines swarmed ashore from the warship *Portsmouth,* hoisted the American flag, declared the town a spoil of war with Mexico, and claimed it for the United States. Two years later, a gold prospector, James W. Marshall, found gold not far away. This discovery on the South Fork of the American River resulted in the Gold Rush of 1849, boosting the population from 500 to around 25,000, and turning the bay into a thriving seaport in which 549 ships dropped anchor in the last months of 1849. A later romantic saw San Francisco "born of the meeting of sea captains and gold seekers." Someone with a gift for colorful phrase named the narrow passage between ocean and bay the "Golden Gate."

Despite six fires, including one in 1850 that destroyed eighteen blocks of buildings in ten hours, and strong earthquakes in 1865 and 1868, the San Francisco of the decade called "the Gay Nineties" was the eighth largest city in the country and biggest on the West Coast, with a quarter of a million residents. The *Baedeker Guide* saw the city "on the whole well and substantially built," but with "fewer large buildings of architectural importance than any other city of its size in the country." Earthquakes were the result of violent shifts of two geologic faults, the Hayward and the San Andreas, which bracketed the city. The larger San Andreas ran northward from Mexico, past Los Angeles, through San Juan Bautista, the Santa Cruz mountains, across the San Francisco Peninsula and offshore from the Golden Gate, then east of Point Reyes Peninsula. The faults marked the boundary of continental plates that were under extreme pressure. When released, the ground above and surrounding them shifted violently. Should a city lie in the zone of such a tremor, resulting damage to structures ranged from none, minor, and moderate to catastrophic. To anyone considering traveling to San Francisco who might have heard of quakes in the 1860s, the *Baedeker* assured that while earthquakes occurred "occasionally," they "are never very destructive." Throughout the second half of the nineteenth century, the city continued to attract seekers of instant fortune, footloose adventurers, and romantics from every part of the United States and across the globe.

While the city of Rome's history had been shaped by a geography offering seven hills, San Francisco had triple that number, from Telegraph Hill rising abruptly from the bay shore to a height of 300 feet, to Russian Hill, Twin Peaks, Mount Davidson (the highest), and the preferred pinnacle of the millionaires of the city, Nob Hill. Structures on these lofty geographical features rested on firm ground and solid rock. Buildings on the waterfront had softer footing, and as the city's need for space grew, new areas were claimed through landfills.

"To make the present site of San Francisco suitable for a large city," the *Baedeker Guide* explained, "an immense amount of work had to be done in cutting down hills and ridges, filling up gullies, and reclaiming the mud flats on the bay." This resulted in formerly barren stretches of sand dunes and rocky hills, wooded valleys, fetid swamps, and lagoons being converted into a bustling, thriving city on portions of land that were man-made.

Beginning at the imposing Ferry Building on the northeast shore, Market Street, the area's principal thoroughfare, was a three-and-a-half-mile straight line to Mission Peaks (925 feet above sea level). It served as the city's commercial heart with the offices of banks and trading firms. Towering above the street was the *Examiner* building, home to the *Examiner* newspaper. Originally owned by gold- and silver-mine entrepreneur George Hearst, whose Spanish-style mansion loomed as one of the grandest of Nob Hill, the paper had moved from a small shop on Sacramento Street to Market

Street. Its city room was visited on occasion by Hearst's son, but sixteen-year-old William Randolph Hearst gave no sign at the time that after he took over the paper in 1887, he would use it to become the master of a journalistic empire that would make him a powerhouse of politics in California and across the nation. The *Examiner's* competitors were the *Call, Bulletin, Chronicle,* and the *Daily News.* Across the bay in the city of Oakland, the *Tribune* and the *Herald* provided daily news reports.

Opposite the *Examiner* building stood Baldwin's Theater and the Academy of Sciences, with its impressive staircase of gray California marble. A little farther, at Eighth Street, was the dome-topped City Hall. At Fifth and Mission Streets was a branch of the U.S. Mint. Commerce flowing in and out of the city included gold and silver, coal, timber, wine, fruit and vegetables, baked goods, wool, rice, sugar, tea, leather, liquor, and anything else that could be made or grown, from the necessities of life to its indulgences.

To proclaim its place as a significant city in 1894, San Francisco had thrown a coming-of-age party. The world was invited to its first great carnival. Called "Opal City," this Mid-winter International Exposition was held in the city's grand Golden Gate Park. "In those days," wrote an historian of the city's growth, "a traveler from any point along the coast between the Mexican and Canadian borders simply asked for a ticket to 'the city' with complete assurance that he would be routed to San Francisco."

Like all great seaport cities, San Francisco catered to the carnal desires of men for whom riches were to be mined from the endless veins of vice that course through the histories of such places. The seeds of vice had first been sown in Portsmouth Square in the form of gambling dens and brothels. They soon spread outward along Pacific Street, from Sansome Street to Grant Avenue. In a waterfront area called the Barbary Coast appeared such enticements as Spider Kelly's, Purcell's, the Comstock, Golden Star, Turkish Café, Moulin Rouge, White House, So Different, Dutch Emma's Squeeze Inn, Cascade, the Admiral, and Owl Dance Hall. Houses of prostitution announced their presence with a red light that glowed from dusk to dawn, and a lamp with a red shade in a front window during the day.

Three kinds of brothels flourished in this red-light district. Depending on the tariff, a customer would patronize a cow-yard, with cubicles for as many as 300 women; a crib, used by streetwalkers; or the parlor house, offering "higher quality" women at premium prices.

Each establishment provided enrichment for Jerome Bassity. No one doing business on the Barbary Coast owned more brothels and saloons. Orphaned at age eight, he'd peddled newspapers, worked as an usher in a theater, and delivered milk to houses in the red-light district. After a madam took a liking to him and set him up in a saloon with upstairs bedrooms, he discerned that the good life for himself could be easily financed by giving the men of San Francisco, visitors and residents alike, what they desired. He told a reporter, "I like the best of everything. The best wine, the best food, the best clothing. It takes money to get them."

"The best of everything:" he might have been describing San Francisco. On the night of April 17, 1906, its population was 450,000. Twice the size of Los Angeles, it was the New York City of the West Coast. As well as being a financial and commercial center, it was a growing city of impressive architecture, with fine hotels, mansions, and residential neighborhoods that were safe, neat, and inviting.

It was also a seat of culture with theaters featuring the biggest stars of the Broadway stage. Dinners before the curtains went up, or suppers after the last curtain called, were served at the restaurant in the Palace Hotel, Tortoni's on O'Farrell Street, Marchand, Wilson's, the Poodle Dog Rotisserie, and Zinkand's Restaurant, famous for its huge servings of spaghetti. The theaters included the California; Stockwell's; the Alcazar; Bush Street Theater; the Columbia, offering Victor Herbert's new musical *Babes in Toyland*; the Tivoli (*Miss Timidity*); and the Baldwin, where John Barrymore, one of the famous Barrymore family of actors, had just closed in a run of *The*

Dictator as the star of a touring theatrical troupe. His next booking was in Australia. With the sailing scheduled for the morning of April 18, he chose to spend his last night in San Francisco at the Grand Opera House on Mission Street near Third Street.

Starring in *Carmen* was the world's greatest tenor, Enrico Caruso. For his appearance as the dashing Don Jose with the Conreid Opera Company of San Francisco, he was being paid $1,350. To sing the role in *Carmen,* Caruso had canceled a trip to Naples, Italy, because of the eruption of the volcano, Mount Vesuvius. Three thousand of San Francisco's opera aficionados would pay from seven dollars to sixty-seven dollars to see and hear him sing.

Covering this social event of the year for the *Call* was reporter James Hopper. Famed as a "tackler" for the Stanford "Imposters" football team, class of 1900, he'd heard a rumor that there had been an argument between Caruso and Madame Olive Fremstad. Fremstad, an amply busted soprano, was playing opposite Caruso as the beautiful, slim, and sexy young girl who made her living wrapping cigars. She and Caruso had argued about the quality of her performance. The diva said that she faltered in her aria because she was upset with the quality of work by the opera house's stagehands. If management had not been paying Caruso so much, she contended, more professional labor could have been hired. The Great Caruso, Hopper had been told, erupted like Vesuvius. If any stagehands were fired because of Madame Fremstad, he warned, he would not go on stage and would never again appear in an opera with the temperamental prima donna.

Noting that the opera management had posted no announcements of changes in the cast of *Carmen,* Hopper was left with an event to report that was far less exciting than a battle of two opera stars. Instead of backstage theatrics, *Call* subscribers would read about the preening of San Francisco's high society. Dressed to the nines, adorned with glittering jewelry, and sporting other trappings befitting the elite of California's recently gained or inherited wealth, they had come down from gilded palaces overlooking the city from an elevated place that the working class scorned as "Snob Hill."

While Hopper observed the arrivals outside the Opera House, the *Call*'s society reporter, Laura Bridge Powers, was within. "The house," she would record, "was a terraced garden of orchids and narcissus and nodding roses, with fruit blossoms scattered between."

Whether Mayor Eugene E. Schmitz would show up for the performance remained to be seen. Known as "Handsome Gene," he was a native San Franciscan. Born on August 24, 1864, he had been a concert violinist, orchestra leader, and president of the Musician's Union. He entered politics at the urging of the city's political boss, Abraham Ruef. Doubts that Schmitz would choose to hear Caruso were based on the fact that Schmitz and Ruef were in deep trouble for having flouted the laws of California against government corruption.

The story bantered about in newspaper city rooms of Schmitz's decision to run for mayor in 1901 as the candidate of the newly-formed Union Labor Party was that Ruef had told a very reluctant Schmitz, "You have as much experience and information as many men who have been nominated, and more than some who have filled the office." Observing that Schmitz was "a man of fine appearance," Ruef offered a cynical view of elections. "The psychology of the mass of voters," he said, "is like that of small boys or primitive men. Other things being equal, of two candidates they will almost invariably follow the strong, finely built man."

With the ardent support of labor unions, the endorsement of "Willie" Hearst's *Examiner,* and Abraham Ruef's skills at political conniving, Schmitz was astonished to find that he was elected. With the distinction of being the first Union Labor mayor in the country, he was also a first step in Ruef's grand design to make the Union Labor Party a national force. Ruef would confide to Schmitz during a meeting in a small hotel tucked into the tranquil hills of Sonoma, California, that Schmitz's victory would be the spark in California that would kindle the entire nation and make a labor president. He saw the Union Party as "a throne for Schmitz, as mayor, as governor–

as President of the United States." The power behind the throne, local, state, and national, would be Ruef himself, ideally from a seat in the U.S. Senate.

Five years and two re-elections later, Schmitz and his wily mentor were rich beyond the imaginations of the working people of San Francisco. An investigation of Schmitz's administration found it built on "an alignment of the citizens, based on bitter class antagonism." This resulted in "ideal conditions for municipal corruption." Voters who chose Schmitz did so because they saw him as their "class representative." They overlooked "the method in which he performs the ordinary functions of his position and are absorbed entirely by those official or extra-official acts which favor or injure the apparent interests of their class."

As the man behind the scene, Abraham Ruef had extended himself beyond civic graft into the "vicious industries of the town" in the form of payoffs by which operators of gambling dens, saloons, and houses of prostitution, including Jerome Bassity, stayed in business without fear of interference by the police. A healthy portion of the money funneled into the pockets of the mayor, and, according to a rumor, into a secret cache under the floorboards of Schmitz's bedroom called a "boodle box." There was a hiding place, Schmitz admitted, but it was for the safe storage of his valuable violin.

The result of investigations by the *Bulletin* into Schmitz and Ruef's alleged corruptions had resulted in an official hearing scheduled for April 18. This may have accounted for the mayor not occupying a box seat in the Opera House on the evening of April 17 to see Caruso stopping the show in Act II with Don Jose's aria, *Il Fior Che Avevi A Me Tu Dato*. Had the mayor attended, he would have read in the program that "Caruso is the most charming and lovable of characters, never shirking rehearsal duties." When Caruso was not singing, noted the program, "his chief delight is sketching caricatures of himself and his acquaintances."

After numerous curtain calls, Caruso found an automobile awaiting him at the stage door to convey him one block to the

Palace Hotel on Market Street for drinks amid the blooms of its garden court. When the maestro was ready to dine, the maitre d' at Zinkand's would bring him, the world's most famous Italian next to the Pope, any dish he requested, whether it was on the menu or not. While he waited for the food to be served, a young piano player named Elsa Maxwell rendered a medley of familiar operatic melodies. A native of San Francisco, Elsa had dreams of one day becoming a renowned hostess in high society, but in New York. Finished with his meal, Caruso lived up to his reputation as a caricaturist. He drew amusing sketches of friends on a tablecloth that was unlikely to ever be sent out for a washing.

Although John Barrymore was booked on a ship bound for Australia that would depart in the morning, he did not go directly from the opera to his hotel, the St. Francis on Powell Street. Where he went remains a mystery. Before the opera, he'd dined at the Oyster Loaf restaurant with *Examiner* drama critic Ashton Stevens with hopes of borrowing money and getting "a modicum of advice for the lovelorn." Stevens said that Barrymore had told him that he was staying with a woman whom he met at the opera. The actor wrote in his autobiography that he retired to the home of a friend to inspect his collection of rare Chinese glass.

Well fed and back in his fifth floor suite of the Palace Hotel at Market and Montgomery, Caruso got ready for bed. He recalled "feeling very contented" because he had sung well and the opera was one "with fine éclat." Everyone had been pleased. He went to sleep "feeling happy."

The opera reviewer for the *Call* was ecstatic. Caruso, he wrote, was a "magician." The Bizet opera had "rechristened itself." For San Francisco's opera season, he said, it was not *Carmen,* but *Don Jose.*

At the *Examiner,* Ashton Stevens, who'd dined on oysters with Barrymore, but without lending him money, turned in his review of Caruso's performance and encountered the prejudice of the paper's owner. Among Willie Hearst's many fixations was a grudge against New York's Metropolitan Opera Company that translated to a reluctance to give any praise to the Met's most illustrious performer, even in faraway San Francisco. When the *Examiner*'s editor, Charles Michelson, proposed that Stevens might be fired if he heaped an excess of plaudits on Caruso, Stevens stood his ground. He exclaimed that there were three weeks left of reviewing the Metropolitan Opera's San Francisco performances and he would write what he believed. On the way out, he blurted, "I hope the god-damned opera house burns down."

With the rafters of the Opera House probably still shaking from the ovation given to the Great Caruso, James Hopper had watched a seemingly countless number of elegant carriages and a smattering of automobiles stream away from the Opera House, turn off Market Street, past the St. Francis Hotel and Union Square, and begin a steep climb on Powell Street to the grandeur of multimillion-dollar mansions and the under-construction Fairmont Hotel. Designed to rest like a crown on the crest of Nob Hill, it would challenge in opulence the homes of the grandees of the city, including the three-story, Gothic-style abode built by Mary Hopkins. Wife of Mark, she had decreed a turreted entrance, a paneled dining room seventy-five-feet long, a ballroom, a library, and a bedroom for herself that had a velvet-padded door and a ceiling festooned with carved angels.

Sauntering to the *Call* building, Hopper was already composing in his head a story that would brim with anecdotes and colorful vignettes of the city's hoi polloi on a stellar night out at the opera. In reporting on events in San Francisco, he was following in the footsteps of a pair of journalistic greats who had tramped the same streets and daunting hills.

From Albany, New York, in 1854, had come Francis Bret Harte to write news stories for *The Californian*, working beside Mark Twain, before being appointed Secretary of the United States Branch Mint at San Francisco, a post he held until 1870.

Between June and October 1864, Twain had been a reporter for the San Francisco *Daily Morning Call*. A year later, he wrote to a friend that he'd "enjoyed my first earthquake." It was just past noon on a bright October day. "I was coming down Third Street," he recalled. "The only objects in motion anywhere in sight in that thickly built and populous quarter, were a man in a buggy behind me, and a street car wending slowly up the cross street. Otherwise, all was solitude and Sabbath stillness. As I turned the corner, around a frame house, there was a great rattle and jar, and it occurred to me that here was an item!–no doubt a fight in that house."

The disturbance, he noted, was not a domestic quarrel, but "the 'great' earthquake, and is doubtless so distinguished till this day." Since 1865, San Francisco had known none like it.

Seated at a typewriter in the city room of the *Call* in what were now the early hours of the morning of Wednesday, April 18, 1906, James Hopper quickly batted out his story. Dropping it onto the desk of the editor, he called it a night. Feeling too restless to sleep, he walked along Market Street toward the waterfront, awash with the excitement that all journalists experience after having turned in a good story. To unwind, he knew of nothing more peaceful than watching the ships coming to and going from the bay, and seeing the red and green lights dotting the long and short silhouettes of those that were docked. He enjoyed imagining their next ports of call and often dreamed that he might one day take one and sail to an exotic spot halfway around the world.

Until that time, if he needed to get away from the city on a boat he could take one of the ferries that criss-crossed the bay. He could make an excursion on one of the ferries through the Golden Gate for the sole purpose of giving tourists an ocean view of the city. After gazing at San Francisco from the sea, Bret Harte had been stirred to write a poem:

> Serene, indifferent of Fate,
> Thou sittest at the Western Gate;
> Upon thy height, so lately won,
> Still slant the banners of the sun;

Thou seest the white seas strike their tents,
O warder of two continents!
And, scornful of the peace that flies
Thy angry winds and sullen skies,
Thou drawest all things, small or great,
To thee, beside the Western Gate.

If an ocean view was not his choice for spending a day off, Hopper might shell out two-and-a-half dollars to go to Sausalito or to Tiburon. From there he could take a train to San Rafael and make a two-and-a-half-hour climb to enjoy a lofty, but fourteen-mile-distant panorama of the city atop Mount Tamalpais. Or he might use his status as a reporter to visit the naval station on Mare Island.

Looking toward the middle of a bay bathed in moonlight, he saw specks of light from the lamps of Alcatraz Island. On such a pleasant April night its prison cells were made even more gloomy because its barred windows provided the men within them views of the free-booting corsairs of the world's seas, and a view of a fabulous city on the opposite shore. For the inmates it had to be a painful reminder of gaudy days and bawdy nights, of the now unattainable delights, in the dens and dives of the Barbary Coast. An earlier writer for the *Call* vividly termed the area north of Market Street from East Street a "sink of moral pollution, whose reefs are strewn with human wrecks, and into whose vortex is constantly drifting barks of moral life, while swiftly down the whirlpool of death go the sinking hulks of the murdered and the suicide."

As far as Jerome Bassity knew while he headed home, there had been no deaths in any of his establishments on the night that Enrico Caruso had sung at the Opera House. Nor had any killings been called to the attention of Sergeant Jesse Cook of the police department while he walked his waterfront beat. South of Market Street, Police Lieutenant H. N. Powell also found nothing to relay to headquarters as he made his rounds in a frequently troublesome neighborhood.

PROLOGUE: *Gaudy Days, Bawdy Nights*

Because no Owl Cars (streetcars) were operating, Thomas Jefferson Chase walked to his job as telegrapher and ticket clerk on the early morning shift at the Ferry Building on First Street. He had to walk down Folsom Street to First, then over to Market Street to his usual spot for having breakfast. But on this morning, he didn't have time to linger. He had overslept in a room he shared with another telegrapher in a private home on Fremont Street. Named Gibbs, he worked the afternoon shift. Irked at being awakened by Chase's alarm clock, and that Chase had not turned it off, he'd shouted at Chase several times and threatened that if Chase didn't get a move on, he would get up and drag him out of bed.

Home for James Hopper was a hotel room on Post Street. Heading there a little before two in the morning, he passed a livery stable and found a stableman trying to quiet horses that were making a terrible racket, rearing up, whinnying, and banging against the sides of the stalls. With a perplexed look at Hopper, the stableman said, "Restless tonight. I don't know why."

Suddenly feeling tired when he entered his room, Hopper threw himself onto his bed.

Three hours later, it moved beneath him. It shook and rocked so violently that he awoke thinking the earth had unleashed a vicious personal attack.

One

RUDE AWAKENINGS

ITH THE HOTEL ROOM QUIVERING AND spinning, James Hopper laid in bed for a moment, his head on the pillow, watching his stretched and stiffened body spring up and down and shift from side to side, as he would describe it, "like a pancake in the tossing griddle of an experienced French chef." When a bureau at the back of the room suddenly lurched toward him in an awkward kind of dance, "in a zigzag course, with sudden bold advances and as sudden bashful retreats–with little bows, and becks, and nods," it seemed funny. Then a chunk of plaster fell from the ceiling and crashed onto his head.

Beginning at 5:13 A.M., Wednesday, April 18, 1906, and lasting forty-seven seconds, the earthquake jolt as recorded by the U.S. Weather Bureau on Post Street was felt over an area of about 375,000 square miles. The ground shook from Coos Bay, Oregon, to Los Angeles, as far east as central Nevada, and across a vast expanse of the Pacific Ocean. Five minutes later, a second tremor rumbled for a few seconds, as did aftershocks at 5:25 and 5:42.

Bounding out of bed, Hopper realized that the whole building could come tumbling down upon him. Loosening bricks sounded like chattering teeth. As his head filled with a panorama of the cataclysm

I

that had befallen Pompeii, the Indonesian volcano Krakatoa, and the recent eruption of Vesuvius, he thought of San Francisco and muttered, "It's the end."

If what was happening in the city, and possibly everywhere else in the world, was the beginning of the Apocalypse as foretold in Holy Scripture, it was the greatest news story that a journalist could ever be handed. Scooping up his reporter's notebook with its pages of scrawled notes about a gala night at the opera, he felt a rush of excitement and dashed for the door. On the street, he looked around at the crumbling buildings and frantic people running for their lives and exclaimed, "Good Lord!"

In a third-floor window of a building on the verge of falling onto a pile of rubble that was the remains of adjoining structures, a man had knotted bed sheets into a makeshift ladder. Dashing atop the small mountain of debris, Hopper yelled, "Wait! I'll help you."

Climbing up, he peered through a shattered window and saw the slim white hand and wrist of a young woman reaching desperately from under a litter of fallen ceiling plaster. After carrying her out, he returned to the building and rescued two more women. Told that someone was buried in the rubble, he joined two men and a pair of firemen who were clawing away bricks and wood. The work ended when another fireman rushed by and grumbled, "What's the use of diggin' out the ones that are dead?"

There was no way of knowing how many bodies lay in the ruins as dawn broke over the shattered city. But the fireman was right, Hopper decided. The only people that mattered were the living. Recalling his discovery that there had been many left alive, Hopper said, "I threw my chest out and looked with amazement upon my dazed co-citizens."

Among the immediately killed was fireman James O'Neill. Drawing water for the horses of Fire Station No. 4 on Howard Street opposite Hawthorne when the quake hit, he was killed by a collapsing wall of the adjacent American Hotel. At almost the same instant, the chief engineer of the fire department, Dennis T. Sullivan, was with his wife Margaret at the Chief's Quarters at 410 Bush Street. When he fell through a ruptured floor into the cellar, the brick chimneys and dome of the California Hotel crashed through the adjoining fire station of Chemical Company No. 3. All hands had been in bed except hoseman Maroney, who was on watch.

"When the crash ended," Battalion Chief Walter A. Cook wrote in an official report, "we started at once to dig for the Chief and Mrs. Sullivan." Men from the San Francisco *Bulletin*, located across the street, assisted them in the effort. To everyone's amazement, Chief Sullivan emerged from the pile of ruins. Mrs. Sullivan was soon rescued and treated for slight injuries amid the wreckage of the hotel. Chief Sullivan suffered a slight skull fracture, badly lacerated right hip, several cracked ribs, and numerous cuts and bruises. But he had also been scalded by steam and water gushing from a radiator. Treated first in the St. George Stables, he was then taken to the hospital of the Southern Pacific railway company, and finally transferred to the army's hospital at the Presidio. He died four days later. Seven other firemen died in the collapsing of a brick powerhouse at Seventh and Valencia Streets.

Eleven blocks away on Valencia, between Eighteenth and Nineteenth Streets, Lieutenant H. N. Powell had paused during his rounds to chat with the night clerk of the Valencia Hotel. He reported finding newspapermen playing cards and sipping beer while the clerk was "behind the desk resting but ready for business" that required him to "put through calls for roomers that had to catch trains or had to get to work early." As Powell left the clerk to his duties, Valencia Street "not only began to dance and rear and roll in waves like a rough sea in a squall, but it sank in places and then vomited up its [street] car tracks and the tunnels that carried the cables." The convulsions caused the two lower floors of the hotel to drop into the cellar and the top floor to pitch into a buckled street that resembled an accordion. Few of the hotel's 120 guests were alive. One survivor was an infant girl, cradled in the arms of her dead father.

After telephoning the supervisors at police headquarters at five o'clock at the end of his overnight beat, Police Sergeant Jesse Cook strolled along Washington Street into the produce district and found it stirring for another day's business of providing the homes and restaurants of a city famed for its cuisine with the required ingredients, to be conveyed to kitchen and pantry doors by horse carts. After talking awhile with the produce area's beat policeman, H. C. Schmitt, Cook stopped for another chat with a young horseback rider who was doing his best to calm his inexplicably jittery horse. When Cook asked what the trouble was, the youth answered, "I don't know. I never saw him act like this before."

Moments after leaving the rider, Cook heard an ominous rumbling and suspected what had spooked the horse. When he saw the cobblestones of Washington Street suddenly move and heard wood creaking and glass breaking, then felt the pavement rumble beneath him, he was certain. The next second, he reeled like a Barbary Coast drunkard. He steadied himself as much as possible, then dashed to the center of the street to avoid collapsing walls. As he raced toward the corner of Washington and Davis Streets, the ground ahead split, forming a six-foot-deep trench that rapidly filled with water from ruptured pipes.

Leaping the gouge, Cook scrambled for a building that he hoped would provide refuge from falling debris, only to find that the shaking had caused a partial collapse. The walls would have come all the way down, he noted, if the doorway hadn't been piled with sturdy produce boxes. Familiar with the nature of earthquakes, he knew to expect that the tremor was the first of what would surely be many. When the second occurred, it was shorter, but seemed much worse. The earth that had been reclaimed from marshland twisted, jerked, and bounced so violently that he feared it would give way altogether and slip into the bay like a child on a sliding board.

Braced in the nearly demolished doorway, Cook could only wonder when the city would shake again with the inevitable tremors that people who knew more about earthquakes than he blithely dismissed as "aftershocks." Convinced that the quake was far from finished, he also wondered how much, if any, of the city was left standing.

A couple of blocks away, Policeman Schmitt gazed in horror from the sheltering arch of a doorway as the front of a three-story building came crashing down through an awning to land in a giant heap in the street. "The dust and debris," he lived to report, "covered my feet and rained a wall of ruin and rubbish in front of me that reached as high as my neck."

Another policeman on patrol in the market district recorded, "The spectacle was pitiable. The fronts of the low buildings on either side of the street between Montgomery and Sansome had fallen out and buried a number of men that were working in the various fish and meat markets at that busy hour. They had also buried and crushed numerous teams and wagons." All he could do for the animals, he said, was shoot them. He noted grimly and sadly, "I must have shot a dozen or more."

Policemen Max Fenner and Percy Smith, working the beat on Mason Street, were killed in the collapse of the Essex Hotel. A niece of a San Francisco Police Department detective named Dillon died in a crumbled building at Sixth Street and Shipley. But patrolman Billy Sbeches was able to rescue three people.

"If the seismic disturbance had occurred in the daytime," a writer would observe in the official organ of the State and Local Building Trades Council of California, *Organized Labor*, "when the busy thoroughfares of the metropolis were lined with people, or in the evening when the theaters were crowded, there would have been still more horrifying chapters in the world's history than the one which the city by the Golden Gate has just contributed."

Crediting "all-wise Providence" for "the most fortunate hour for the appalling catastrophe," the account continued:

> The first heavy shock, a few minutes after five in the morning, struck terror to the bravest and coolest of the city's sleeping

populace. In a few seconds the streets in the residence districts were lined with people who rushed out of their apartments and homes in night attire. Furniture, pianos, book cases danced through the rooms as if possessed with demons; crockery and china were dashed out of their closets on the floors; chimneys toppled over and houses cracked and caved in.

One that evidently did not crumble into a heap of wreckage was the house of the friend to which John Barrymore said he ventured after attending the opera to admire the friend's collection of Chinese glassware. Awakened by the jolt, he heard the friend painfully plead, "Come and see what has happened to my Ming Dynasty."

What the youngest member of an American dynasty of actors said in consolation can only be surmised. With condolences presumably expressed, Barrymore put on the white tie and tails he'd worn the previous night, donned his opera cape, and departed to keep an appointment with a ship that was to carry him to Australia. Arriving at the St. Francis Hotel to pick up his luggage, he encountered the manager of his acting troupe. Barrymore greeted William Collier with, "What's up, Willie?"

"Nothing's up at all," replied Collier. "In fact, everything is down." He continued with a reference to New York newspaper mogul Horace Greeley's often-quoted advice to a youth to test the glorious prospects to be found far beyond the Appalachian Mountains. Greeley had said, "Go West, young man." Collier said, "Go West, young man, and blow up the country."

Opposite the St. Francis in Union Square, a memorial to the naval hero of the Spanish-American War, Admiral George Dewey, whose defeat of Spain's Pacific fleet in Manila Bay in the Philippines had won the islands for the United States, was a ruin. Its iron columns were bent to the ground and twisted like strands of wire.

Staying in the Maryland Hotel across the street from Dewey's tribute, A. D. Evans of New Brunswick, New Jersey, had been hurled out of bed in his third-floor room. Covered with plaster from the ceiling, he'd rescued two women who were trapped in their room and reached the street along with hundreds of hotel guests in all stages of dress and undress. When he looked toward the building of the *Call*, looming in the distance, he gaped in amazement at a burst of greenish flame from its sixth floor. In the next instant, the building was a mass of flames from top to bottom. Of that early morning Evans would relate:

> As there was no apparent indication of further harm, and as the Maryland Hotel was still intact, I ran back to the building and into my room. I put on my clothing and took my money from my trunk. I then went downstairs again.
>
> Passing through the halls of the hotel I saw groups of men and women sitting on the floor, and in every conceivable attitude of distress and helplessness. No one seemed to know what to do.
>
> I went to the hotel proprietor, who was trying to reassure the guests, and was talking to him when there was another tremor of the earth, and with it people in the hotel made a mad rush for the street. In this one woman was killed and three were so badly injured that they died later in Union Square.

A guest in the Grand Hotel said that the first shock had shaken the hotel "as a terrier would shake a rat." When he fled to the street, it seemed to move "like waves of water." On his way down Market Street he saw dead people "piled up in an automobile like carcasses in a butcher's wagon, all over blood, with crushed skulls and broken limbs, and bloody faces." When he reached the ferry docks with the hope of taking a ferry across the bay to Oakland, the ground was gaping in places. As women and children knelt and prayed aloud for God's mercy, looming over them was the amazingly intact tower of the Ferry Building, although the south wall of the building had crashed through a driveway into the bay.

On his way to grab a bit of breakfast en route to work at the

Ferry Building, Thomas Jefferson Chase had gotten about halfway to Howard Street on the west side of First Street when he heard a distant rumbling, growing louder and louder from the west. Suddenly, power and trolley lines snapped like threads, then hissed and writhed on the ground like snakes.

When the shock stopped, Chase crossed First Street, only to be knocked down by the second shock onto cobblestones that danced like corn kernels in a popper. In a shower of brick and glass, he got to his feet and started for Howard Street. By the time he reached the corner and the site of an old structure known as the Selby Shot Tower, the ground was again shaking. As he scrambled away from the tower, he expected it to fall. When it remained upright, he gazed up in disbelief at the flagpole, which was snapping like a whip.

He speculated that if the tower had fallen, he would have been crushed. Chase recalled:

> No street was clear through to Market Street until a couple of blocks west of the Embarcadero. When I got to Market Street I noticed the pavement had disappeared. I went back and around and saw that the pavement had dropped fully five feet. The cable slots were compressed until they looked like a solid piece of steel all the way between the rails. I finished my trip to the Ferry Building in the middle of the street. It was safer there. The waves were lazily lapping at the pilings as if nothing had happened.
>
> The boats had backed out into the clear and were coming back into the slips again. One gentleman was there and I asked if he thought we could go to work. We went into the office and found the counters and floor covered with plaster. Everything was wet from broken pipes, but water had stopped running as the mains had been broken along the line. A captain came in and sized up the situation. We decided to get busy and busy it was. We got the first boat out around 6:20, only 20 minutes late; then we resumed normal schedule.

Then I tried the telegraph and telephone lines. They were dead. I wanted to try to get to my mother in Oakland as I feared for her safety; and also wanted to get the office at Oakland Pier. I had no idea the cable would be out of commission, but it was. By 7:00 A.M. the crowds were coming in.

The crowds were gathering fast in the Embarcadero, carrying bundles, suitcases and anything to gather up a few belongings. They began dropping them on the pavement while waiting to go out. The pile grew until it was like a hay stack. It was started just west of the car tracks on the Embarcadero where the Mission [Street] cars stopped. The people all seemed to be dazed or stunned.

Wooden walls of buildings of the fish market, with its popular alfresco restaurants and open-air displays of seafood, game, fruits, and meats, had splintered and were strewn like pick-up sticks. Some docks and freight sheds along the waterfront slid into the bay. The long wharf of the Southern Pacific railway collapsed. Shattered coal-bunkers unleashed their contents into the water. Deep fissures opened in the filled-in ground near the shore.

Spreading out from the Ferry Building, buildings small and great, of wood, brick, and stone, had been ripped apart. One of the first was the city's tallest. On the same side of Market Street as the Palace Hotel, the Spreckels Building was sixteen stories tall. Home to the *Call*, it was topped by a dome of imposing proportions that afforded a breathtaking view of the city. Close by and also wrecked was William Randolph Hearst's *Examiner* building. Other landmark buildings left in ruins were those of the Pacific Mutual Life Insurance Company, the Phelan Building at the juncture of Market and O'Farrell Streets, Western Union Telegraph at Pine and Montgomery Streets, Pacific States Telephone, the Natoma Building, and the Nevada Bank Building.

Between Seventeenth and Nineteenth Streets, from Dolores to Protrero, everything was shattered, as were buildings in the neighborhood bounded by Mission, Seventh, Harrison, and Fourth Street.

Most of the older structures on Montgomery Street and east along the waterfront were cracked. At Sixth and Howard, the five-story, 300-room Brunswick Hotel crashed down. Luckier was the large Cosmopolitan House at Fifth and Mission, suffering the fall of only one portion. But the destruction of the Portland House between Mission and Market left about sixty people buried and crying for help. While most were dragged out alive, others were being rescued from the Royal, a lodging house at Fourth and Mission. More lucky ones escaped from what one reporter coined "the human beehives," the Lick House and the Russ House north of Market Street. But few were saved from the heaped remains of the eighty rooms of the four-story Wilson House at 775 Mission Street. At the Luxembourg at Stockton and O'Farrell, all but one man and one woman managed to avoid being crushed under tons of falling brick from an adjoining building. Withstanding the quake were the relatively new Hibernian Bank and the old Dolores Mission, the first building erected by the founding Spanish priests.

The first shocks that sent a mighty wave sweeping through the earth, a chronicler of the devastation wrote, "touched the giant steel structures and left them dangling like broken skeins of yarn above their cracked and broken foundations." Statues that had been the pride of the city toppled and smashed. Church steeples trembled and plummeted "like giant spears."

The tremors that rumbled under the Palace Hotel had swelled its outer walls and the sides of its grandiose inner courtyard as if the magnificent hostelry for theatrical personalities and grand opera stars was made of paper. On the fifth floor at 5:13 that morning, Enrico Caruso thought he was dreaming that he was on a ship crossing the ocean on the way to his beautiful Italy. Waking, he realized his bed was rocking as if it was a boat. When the motion continued, he got out of bed, went to a window, and raised the shade. In a narrative for the London magazine *The Sketch*, reprinted in the July 1906 issue of *The Theater* magazine, accompanied by his own drawings as illustrations, he wrote:

And what I see makes me tremble with fear. I see the buildings toppling over, big pieces of masonry falling, and from the street below I hear the cries and screams of men and women and children.

I remain speechless, thinking I am in some dreadful nightmare, and for something like forty seconds I stand there, while the buildings fall and my room still rocks like a boat on the sea. And during that forty seconds I think of forty thousand different things. All that I have ever done in my life passes before me, and I remember trivial things and important things. I think of my first appearance in grand opera, and I feel nervous about my reception, and again I think I am going through last night's Carmen. And then I gather my faculties together and call for my valet. He comes rushing in quite cool, and without any tremor in his voice, says, "It is nothing."

This assurance expressed, the valet advised Caruso to "dress quickly and go into the open, lest the hotel fall and crush us to powder." He was handed clothing, and he paid no attention to what he was given. As he put on trousers, socks, shoes, and a coat, the room shook again. "Then we run down the stairs and into the street," he remembered, "and my valet, brave fellow that he is, goes back and bundles all my things into trunks and drags them down six flights of stairs and out into the open one by one. While he is gone for another and another, I watch those that have already arrived, and presently someone comes and tries to take my trunks, saying they are his. I say, 'No, they are mine'; but he does not go away. Then a soldier comes to me; I tell him that this man wants to take my trunks, and that I am Caruso, the artist who sang in *Carmen* the night before. He remembers me and makes the man who takes an interest in my baggage 'skiddoo,' as Americans say."

Making his way to Union Square, Caruso found Metropolitan Opera colleagues who had been staying at the St. Francis, other nearby hotels, and rooms in private residences. An observer noted that prima donnas escaped in nightdresses and world-famous tenors, bassos, and baritones emerged from wrecked hotels in pajamas to mingle with unknown people by the hundreds. The differences of class and background, nationality, and languages were forgotten as someone passed out bread and sardines. One barefooted musician, wearing only his underwear, clutched his violin. A singer blurted to Caruso that he'd lost everything but his voice. He urged Caruso to go with him to a house that was still standing. "No," said Caruso. "I prefer to remain in a place where there is no fear of being buried by falling buildings." While the valet fetched trunks, he chose to "lie down in the square for a little rest," convinced the earthquake had some relation to the eruption of Vesuvius.

Madame Olive Fremstad, who had been staying at the small but elegant St. Dunstan Hotel, brushed aside pleas from friends that she leave the neighborhood and remained through the day and night, helping the injured, comforting others, and buying food and wine for all.

None of the Metropolitan Opera's singers and musicians had any way of knowing as they mingled with their colleagues and strangers who had become refugees that before sunset the scenery and costumes for the company's three weeks in San Francisco would be gone in flames and the magnificent Grand Opera House burned out.

Two

"FOR GOD'S SAKE, SHOOT ME!"

*M*ONTHS EARLIER, MERCHANT PETER Bacigalupi had noted with satisfaction that after it was announced that Enrico Caruso would be performing in San Francisco there had been an upsurge in sales of the tenor's phonograph records at his music emporium. One of the city's most successful retailers, he also owned penny arcades at the same address, one on Market Street, and another in the famed Bella Union Theatre on Kearny Street on the edge of the Barbary Coast. He also operated a wholesale warehouse that made available hundreds of phonographs, pianos, and slot machines to other retailers.

Awakened at quarter past five from a sound slumber by a terrific trembling that he likened to being on the back of a bucking bronco, Bacigalupi sat up in a bed that was going up and down in four directions at once. Amidst the noise of people screaming and wailing and the crashing of chinaware in the parlor of his house, he found himself fascinated by a clock performing "a fancy stunt on the mantel." Despite several chunks of ceiling falling around him, he stayed in bed until the shaking ceased, then dressed in a hurry with the thought that the earthquake must have caused a great deal of damage downtown.

Because no streetcars were running, he walked. When he arrived about eight blocks from the businesses along Market Street, he discovered the havoc wreaked by "this sleeping giant." Not a pane of plate glass remained in display windows. Buildings were tumbled onto their sides and others looked like they had been chopped with a meat cleaver. A few were on fire. With a horrifying vision of smashed phonograph records strewn throughout his store, Bacigalupi tried to hurry on Market Street toward the establishment, but was hindered by terrified people going the other way and, as he would recall, "taking to the hills." Some dragged trunks. Others had valises in their hands or hoisted onto their shoulders. One woman dashed past carrying only an ironing board and a flatiron. Another had a parrot cage in one hand and grasping a bundle of clothing in the other.

Reaching Seventh Street, Bacigalupi observed that Mission Street, a block from Market Street, was in flames. At Sixth Street, he saw a massive wall of fire. Breaking into a run, he dashed across Mission Street, dodging a few automobiles that had been pressed into service as ambulances, and raced to his store at Fourth and Mission. Opposite it, a new six-story building, lately finished and never occupied, was ablaze from ground to roof. He gazed in horror for a moment, then saw another sheet of flames bearing down the side of the street where his store was located. Rushing to it, he found some of his employees waiting on the sidewalk. He tried to unlock the front door, but the latch was too hot to hold. One of the workers pointed out that the glass of a show window was in pieces on the pavement.

After climbing through the opening into the store, Bacigalupi and the others started moving phonograph machines from the front to the rear of the store, believing that if the fire got to the store they could be saved. Accounts and order books were shoved into a large basket and also taken to the back of the store. Other valuable books and papers were left in a safe.

With everything on the ground level moved, Bacigalupi switched his attention and fears to the second floor's phonograph-record salesroom. Reaching the top of the stairs, he gasped in amazement. Not a disc was out of place. He would write of "seeing every record standing on its shelf in perfect order," as though there had been no earthquake. It was, he wrote, "the greatest wonder to me of all—to think that pianos had been thrown down on their faces, and records, which stood by the thousands on our shelves, had not been moved."

Moving to the third floor, which had just been plastered and fixed up as a showroom for musical instruments, he felt a blast of heat from the front of the store. Alone on the floor, he shoved several pianos as far back into the long room as possible. After locking the door to the room to prevent a draft, he went to the fourth and fifth floors and closed and locked their doors. Proceeding to the roof of the building, he felt his stomach sink. Flames were shooting out of the roof of the adjoining building.

Recalling this ghastly sight, he wrote, "As soon as I got there I saw how hopeless was my chance of saving our building from the fire, which was then burning in front. It was consuming a building on either side of us, and as I stood there I saw the flames break through the roof [of the next building], and attack our walls. When I turned around to go down the fire escape at the back of the building, I saw that the fire was also coming on the opposite side of the alley, on which the back entrance of our store faced. The fire was consuming a row of frame buildings, which had stood for years and years, and were now burning like so much paper. The fire was so hot that I decided it was better for us to get away. The basket containing our books and papers we shoved from Mission Street to our penny arcade, which was on Market Street, and which we did not think for a moment was in any danger of fire."

The city's main thoroughfare was a scene of hubbub and confusion. Automobiles that were turned into makeshift ambulances raced back and forth at forty to fifty miles an hour, carrying the wounded and the dead, making crossing Market Street a dangerous enterprise. Finally on the other side of the street and in front of the penny arcade, Bacigalupi felt his stomach sink again as he found great stacks of clothing taken into the streets by frantic storeowners. Inside his penny arcade establishment, he was so overcome with despair that he sank into an office chair and gazed helplessly at his music emporium across the street. As it appeared to be withstanding the fire, his employees offered cheering words. But the fire kept coming, reaching Market Street opposite the penny arcade, and the heat became so fierce that they had to move again. Lugging the basket of papers and account books, he and eight of his staff went to the store of a friend of his a few blocks away. "We could not carry them any farther if we wanted to," he recalled, "as we were all tired out."

His eyewitness account, published several months later in a phonograph-record trade magazine, *Victrola and 78 Journal*, provided remarkably candid evidence of how he'd succeeded as a businessman for thirty-five years, and why even a developing catastrophe appeared to offer opportunity. He wrote:

> The same morning of the earthquake, while standing across the street from the fire, I saw a merchant of the city, who was sobbing as though he were in mortal agony. I was feeling pretty bad at the time, but could not help asking him what his troubles were. He said, "Don't you see the fire right next to my store? I have $10,000 that I will lose if my store is burned."
>
> I thought that I saw a chance for a store in a good location, and offered him $500 for the lease of his place just as it stood, and after much thinking and deliberation, he refused my offer. While we stood there fifteen minutes later his place was burning fiercely.

Bacigalupi lost all his stores and the wholesale operation. Material he thought would be secure in the safe was also lost, turned to ash from the heat. But after a few months, he reported that he was back in business. Dealing in real estate, he said he was "also interested in a restaurant, cigar stand and most important of all–the phonograph business." He'd opened a new store that was much smaller in comparison to the destroyed store. Being in a central location, it was an ideal place "in which to retail talking machines of all the leading types." He was also "putting up my own building on leased ground, two blocks from here, in which to conduct the business of jobbing Edison Phonographs." He'd found starting over "hard," but had taken his two sons into the firm and expected to be able "to do a better and larger business in talking machines than has ever been done in the West."

At the conclusion of his memoir of the earthquake and fire, he wrote, "Regardless of all those ordeals I AM GOING TO STICK WITH 'FRISCO."

Fifty-nine years before Peter Bacigalupi vainly tried to save his music store from flames, the mayor of the bayside village called Yerba Buena had formally changed the name to honor the sainted founder of the Franciscan order of monks. Two days later, the 500 residents of San Francisco grabbed buckets, jars, pots, and anything that held water to battle a brushfire that imperiled fifty-three wooden structures and twenty-six adobe huts. The year after the discovery of gold at Sutter's Mill in the nearby Sierra Mountains, a boomtown of six thousand people fought another blaze that evidently had been started by a gang of bandits who had immigrated from Australia and called themselves the Sydney Ducks. Rebuilt, the town was the victim of arson again in 1850 and 1851. Throughout the 1860s, other blazes were suspected of having been set by competing groups of fire-fighting volunteers.

These frequently violent encounters resulted in the formation of a professional San Francisco Fire Department in 1866. Its record for putting out fires before they became conflagrations had earned it a reputation as one of the finest in the country. But on April 18, 1906, the city's brigades found themselves called upon to extinguish hundreds of fires all over the downtown area known as "South of Market Street," with virtually every water main having been ruptured by the earthquake.

Water to that area was supplied by a city reservoir known as University Mound. Other reservoirs were the Sunol Filter beds in Alameda County, College Hill (elevation 255 feet, near Mission Street and Park Avenue), and at San Andreas and San Mateo, eight miles to the west of Millbrae. With a thirty-seven-and-a-half-inch pipeline, it fed into the city by way of a 500-foot-high trestle. The Sunol system's pipes were on the bottom of the bay. This complex water system included a clay-core dam at San Andreas and a concrete one at San Mateo (the Upper Crystal Springs Dam). The man in charge of the water supply was City Superintendent Thomas G. Packham.

When one of his assistants, Victor Elmo Perry, was rousted from bed by the earthquake, he made his way to Packham's home, but learned that he had already left for the Clarendon Heights pumping station. Although only an easily-repairable steam pipe had broken, the pumps were left useless because the pipes that carried the water to the area served by the station were broken. Unable to reach reservoirs and pumping stations by telephone, Perry and Packham set out by horse and buggy to survey damage to the system. Breaks were found in mains everywhere. Sections of streets had collapsed and become overflowing pools or huge geysers. In some places, men were laboring to close the breeches.

Finding College Hill Reservoir in good condition, Packham and Perry established their headquarters to coordinate repairs. But they quickly learned of severe damage to the pipelines from the outlying reservoirs. Without them, and because of the ruptured mains, city reservoirs would quickly empty, leaving the fire department with little or no water to fight the massive and rapidly advancing fire.

To Thomas Jefferson Chase inside the Ferry Building, the street seemed like a furnace. Flames and smoke rolled with the draft created by the intense heat, moved up the street with a roar, and shot upward hundreds of feet. "It was an awful sight," he remembered. "It was not long until the buildings along the Embarcadero were ablaze. Then the fire jumped Market Street. A little wisp of smoke curled up from a window casing on one of the floors of the old Terminal Hotel on the north side of Market, then other buildings on both sides of the Terminal. Within a half-hour's time Market Street was going good. It was not long until all avenues of escape were cut off from the Ferry Building. Hose lines had been run through the Ferry Building and across driveways to the Embarcadero. A bucket of water would have done as much good. This was for only a short time as the heat became so intense no one could get close enough to do any good. The water just went up in steam and they [firemen] had to give up."

Although businessman Jerome B. Clark's house in Berkeley had been shaken by the quake, there was no damage. Expecting that the tremor had been minor everywhere, he'd boarded his usual cross-bay ferry to go to his office in the city. But when he stepped from the boat, he found "flames were seething" in every direction from the Ferry Building. As he gazed with astonishment, he watched a five-story building half a block away fall with a crash. His account continued:

> The flames swept clear across Market Street and caught a new fireproof building recently erected. The streets in places had sunk three or four feet. In others great humps had appeared four or five feet high. The streetcar tracks were bent and twisted out of shape. Electric wires lay in every direction. Streets on all sides were filled with brick and mortar.
>
> Fires were blazing in all directions, and all of the finest and best of the office and business buildings were either burning or surrounded. They pumped water from the bay, but the fire was soon too far away from the waterfront to make efforts in this direction of much avail. The water mains had been broken by the earthquake, and so there was no supply for the fire engines and they were helpless.

Sparked by hot coals that spilled from stoves onto wooden floors as old buildings shook, the fires quickly found furniture, drapes, and anything else ignitable and leapt to walls and up to ceilings, becoming torches that lit one building after another, leaping between them, and grew and grew and grew. Unrestrained, voracious, and urged to greater fury by breezes off the bay, it was a conflagration for the history books, along with Nero's Rome; the great fires of London in 1666, Washington, D.C. in 1814, and New York City in 1835; the torching of Atlanta by Union soldiers under General William T. Sherman; the Great Chicago Fire of 1871 (which legend blamed the restlessness of Mrs. O'Leary's cow); and fires in Boston in 1872 and Baltimore in 1904.

On an inexorable march inland the fire devoured the cow yards, cribs, and parlor houses of Jerome Bassity and other flesh peddlers with the same fervor as flames that consumed the year-old, four-million-dollar Flood Building. With them went the new Merchants' Exchange, the Crocker Building, Mills Building, and Shreve Building. Along with Peter Bacigalupi's record store and penny arcades went department stores: the Emporium, Hales & Frager's, the White House, O'Connor & Moffatt's, Newman & Levinson's, Roos Brothers', Raphael's, the Hub, the Davis, City of Paris, Samuel's, Vel Strauss', Wallace's, and Bullock and Jones.

Nor would banks be spared: California National, First National, First Canadian Bank of Commerce, the London and San Francisco, Bank of British North America, German-American Savings Bank, and the London, Paris & American Bank all went down with the flames.

In the fire's line of attack were splendid apartment houses with Old World names: Savoy, Plymouth, Abbey, Aberdeen, Granada, Alexandria, and Victoria; and those with "good old" American and Californian names: Colonial, Loma Vista, Buena Vista, and Gotham.

That night San Franciscans would not dine at the Pup, Marchand's, the Poodle Dog, the Fiesta, the famous Palace Hotel grill, the Bohemian resorts of the old part of the city, in the alfresco seafood places of the waterfront, or Zinkand's, where a tablecloth and its sketches by Caruso were food for the hungry flames.

Caruso was forced out of the Palace and into Union Square when hotel after hotel caught fire. After fleeing the Palace, a nationally prominent horseman, R. A. Cole, exclaimed, "My God! I never saw anything like it. And I have seen things, too; I was in the St. Louis cyclone and the Baltimore fire. They were nothing. I saw all San Francisco staggering and rocking and then in flames. I wanted to rush down and jump in the bay and shut out all the awful sights."

Mrs. Mary Longstreet was on the eighth floor of the St. Francis. Looking out a window, she saw the city burning. "In all directions and as far as we could see," she said, "the great tongues of flames leaped into the sky. It was a beautiful, yet terrible sight."

Having fled from a three-story rooming house, Margaret Underhill of Chicago had just missed being crushed in bed by the falling chimney of a building of the adjacent Sacred Heart College. As she and friends made a camping place that seemed safe from the westward-moving fire, they paused to watch firemen, policemen, and several soldiers working furiously at the front of a collapsed and flaming building to free a man buried to his neck. Underhill recalled:

> His head and shoulders projected from the wreckage. With his free arm he tried to help the workers by pulling at the timbers. His eyes bulged from their sockets. One by one the men were driven back by the approaching flames until at last one, a soldier, remained. His face was blistered by the heat.
>
> "Good-bye," the soldier shouted, as a sheet of flame swept around the corner of the building.
>
> The place was one roaring hell. The soldier picked up his rifle, which was standing against a broken timber, and turned to go. From where we stood we could see the very timber that held the man down smoke. His hair and mustache were singed.
>
> "For God's sake, shoot me!" he begged. His voice rose clear above the roar of the flames.
>
> The soldier turned and went back to within twenty-five feet of the man and said something. I could not hear what he said. Then he started to walk away.
>
> "Shoot me before you go," the man yelled. The soldier turned quickly. His rifle was at his shoulder. The rifle cracked

and the blood spurted from the head of the man. I covered my eyes and walked on.

On the south side of Market Street from Ninth Street to the bay, the flames leapt from building to building. Old structures were kindling for fires that attacked adjacent new ones. The sparks from all were carried to others. One report described great mountains of flames that "rose high in the heavens, or rushed down some narrow street, joining midway between the sidewalks and making a horizontal chimney of the former passageways. The dense smoke, which arose from the entire business district, spread out like an immense funnel and could be seen for miles out at sea. Occasionally, as some drug house or place stored with chemicals was reached, most fantastic effects were produced by the colored flames and smoke which rolled out against the darker background."

Not for ninety-five years, when terrorists hatefully perverted a religion and flew hijacked airliners into New York's World Trade Center Twin Towers on September 11, 2001, would American citizens experience the numbing shock and horror of people running to escape the collapsing of prized buildings while an ugly plume of smoke rose above a magnificent harbor and seemed to signify the death of a place that its people had proudly called an "empire city."

Three

❁

DESTROYING FORCES OF NATURE

❁

*S*OLDIERS AT THE PRESIDIO CALLED
Brigadier General Frederick Funston "Freddy." He
was forty-one years old, with red-hair, a neat mus-
tache and Van Dyke beard, and five-feet, four-inches tall. A tough
veteran of the Spanish-American War, he had earned the Congressional Medal of Honor for his exploits in the fight by the U.S. Army
to suppress a rebellion in the Philippines. Enlisted men liked and
admired him because he'd once apologized to a private for blaming
him, erroneously and in front of the man's unit, for some misdeed.

Because Major General Adolphus W. Greely, the commander
of the U.S. Army's Pacific Division, Department of California, was
away from headquarters to attend his daughter's wedding in
Chicago, Funston, as senior officer, was in charge of all military
posts on or near San Francisco Bay. The units consisted of about
1,700 men in ten companies of coast artillery (First, Ninth, and
Twenty-fourth batteries of field artillery); the Twenty-second infantry regiment (Troops I, K, and M); Fourteenth Cavalry; and Company B, Hospital Corps. They were based at the Presidio and Fort
Mason. The Pacific Division's headquarters was downtown, in the
Phelan Building on Market Street.

A family man, General Funston resided at 1310 Washington
Street in what he described as "one of the most elevated parts of the

city." Awakened by the shaking of his home, he had no doubt that an earthquake had occurred. He chose to put on civilian clothes rather than fiddle with the brass buttons and belt of a uniform, and hurried to get a loftier view of the city from California Street. At the pinnacle of Nob Hill, he was afforded a panorama of columns of smoke above the South of Market area. More smoke spiraled up from the banking district. With no streetcars running, he hastened afoot down California to Sansome and found firemen engaged in a hopeless fight due to a lack of water, although it was bubbling up in gallons per second from broken mains. Recognizing "a great conflagration was inevitable," and that the city's police force would not be able to maintain the fire lines and protect public and private property in such a wide area, he ordered out all available troops, "not only for the purpose of guarding federal buildings, but to aid the police and fire departments."

Learning that the telephone system was "prostrated," he realized that he must "return to the first principles" in order to communicate with the commanders at the nearest army posts, the Presidio and Fort Mason. Among the first of the principles was to commandeer a means of quick transportation to the Phelan Building. But without the impressive accoutrements of a general's uniform, he found his efforts to stop passing automobiles futile. He recalled, "Several men dashing wildly about in automobiles declined to assist me, for which I indulged in the pious hope that they'd be burned out."

Alternately running and walking about a mile, he arrived at an army stable on Pine Street and found a soldier driving a carriage assigned to the second-in-command of the California Department. Out of breath and weak in the knees from running, he commanded the soldier to saddle a horse. While that was being done, he scribbled an order to Colonel Charles Morris, an artillery officer who was in command at the Presidio. It directed him to report with his entire command to the city's chief of police at the Hall of Justice on Portsmouth Square. A like message was also to be delivered verbally by the same messenger to Captain M. L. Walker, in command at Fort Mason. A police officer was told to rush to the Hall of Justice and advise the chief of these orders. Leaving the stable, Funston returned to the summit of Nob Hill, "whence could be obtained a good view to the south and east across the great city doomed to destruction."

Funston observed:

> The streets were filled with people with anxious faces, all turned toward the dozen or more columns of thick black smoke rising from the densely populated region south of Market Street. The thing that at this time made the greatest impression on me was the strange and unearthly silence. There was no talking, no apparent excitement among the nearby spectators, while from the great city lying at our feet there came not a single sound, no shrieking of whistles, no clanging of bells.
>
> It was a beautiful clear morning with no wind, and the sinister columns of smoke mounted a thousand feet in the air before they were dissipated. Probably none of the people who watched the imposing spectacle on that occasion would have believed that within thirty-six hours the spot where they stood would be a maelstrom of fire.

Walking to his home, just four blocks away, Funston gave hasty instructions to his family about packing trunks and leaving the house. He changed into his uniform and walked to the Phelan Building. Awaiting him were several officers of the Army's Pacific Division and the Department of California. He informed them that in the absence of General Greely they would take orders from him. Because of his military experience in dealing with instances of public disruption and his familiarity with the city's history as a haven for rough, lawless, and greedy individuals, and criminal gangs, his immediate concern was that the Army assist the city's police in maintaining law and order and preventing looting. When the first detachment of troops arrived from the Engineer Corps at Fort Mason a little before seven o'clock, with full cartridge belts and fixed bayonets, he directed them to stand guard, two to each block, along Market Street. Their orders were to "shoot instantly any person caught looting or committing any serious misdemeanor."

As Enrico Caruso learned when a man attempted to make off with the opera star's trunks, San Francisco was well stocked with crafty individuals eager to exploit someone's vulnerability. Like ports the world over throughout the history of seafaring, the city was a magnet for rough characters from the outset. Then came the discovery of gold and a subsequent rush to find more by a flood of migrants known as "Forty Niners," most of whom soon found that their dreams of instant riches would not pan out, leaving them to find other means of living, including criminality. As the city expanded and its population grew, the lawless underclass kept pace. In dark corners of the city, noted a city historian, were hideouts of such vicious gangs as the Hounds and the Sydney Ducks. They preyed on other thugs and respectable citizens alike, leading to the formation in 1851 of a Vigilance Committee of several thousand members who took the law into their own hands, including hangings without benefit of trials. Four years later, the city was again swarming with miscreants and felons. On April 18, 1906, the legacy of this history could be found in the saloons, gambling dens, prostitution establishments, and other emporiums of vice of the Barbary Coast and the waterfront. Denizens of these places were defined by police as "wharf rats," and while the earth shook that morning they swarmed out to see what profit could be made wherever they found a shattered display window of a store inviting them to enter and pillage merchandise, by sticking up a terrified individual who might have a wallet or purse, pocket-picking among people as they mingled in parks that became refugee camps, making off with the luggage of guests such as Caruso who had been evicted by the quaking of hotels and houses, and scavenging like ghouls for the money and valuables of the trapped, the wounded, the dying, and the dead in the rubble of collapsed and burning buildings.

A telegram by Funston to the Military Secretary in Washington reported, "We are doing all possible to aid residents of San Francisco in present terrible calamity. Many thousands homeless. I shall do everything in my power to render assistance, and trust to War Department to authorize any action I might have to take."

Funston sent a messenger with an order for Colonel Alfred Reynolds, commander of the Twenty-second Infantry at Fort Mc-Dowell on Angel Island, directing his men to embark at once and land at the foot of Market Street, then march to the Phelan Building for assignment. In the meantime, clerks and messengers in the headquarters worked to preserve the records of the department in its fourth-floor offices.

Troops without horses and coast artillerymen arrived from the Presidio a little before eight o'clock. As they were receiving orders at 8:14, the Phelan Building was violently shaken by the first shock since 5:42. Although this one lasted only five seconds, it was the most severe since the initial tremor at 5:13. Alexander McAdie at the Weather Bureau in the Mills Building would note more aftershocks at 9:13, 9:25, 10:49, 11:05, 12:03, 12:10, 2:25, 2:27, 4:50, 6:49, and 7:00. No further records of the smaller quakes would be made at the bureau because the Mills Building caught fire. While McAdie was unable to save his instruments, he established communication with Washington, D.C., by using equipment that belonged to W. R. Eckart. Living next door to McAdie's home on Clay Street, Eckart was a consulting engineer for Union Iron Works. He had a complete set of weather apparatus; consequently, his house became the U.S. Weather Bureau, from which McAdie was able to note later aftershocks and to forecast that heavy showers could be expected during the remainder of Wednesday, but the city and its environs would then enjoy a period of pleasant weather.

Headquarters and First Battalion, Twenty-second Infantry, arrived from Fort McDowell by boat at ten o'clock. General Funston held them in reserve at O'Farrell Street, and then used them in patrols to assist the fire department. At about 10:05, the DeForest Wireless Telegraph Station in San Diego signaled a report of the San

Francisco crisis to the *U.S.S. Chicago*. Admiral Capsar Goodrich ordered the ship to get underway and proceed north at full speed. This event entered the annals of the U.S. Navy as the first use of wireless telegraphy in a natural disaster.

Commanded by Lieutenant Frederick Newton Freeman, the *U.S.S. Preble* sailed from Mare Island at 10:30 to land a hospital shore party at the foot of Howard Street to assist the staff at Harbor Emergency Hospital. Also rushing to the city on Funston's demand were troops from Alcatraz Island, Fort Baker in Marin County, the Presidio of Monterey (about 100 miles south of San Francisco), and Vancouver Barracks near Portland, Oregon.

As an army general, Funston knew that under the Constitution of the United States the only person empowered to order federal forces into action on American soil and possibly against American citizens was the president or a designee. Certainly, no mere brigadier general was permitted to impose martial law. The last time troops stood against U.S. civilians had been during a railway strike in Chicago, when President Grover Cleveland sent an army unit to guarantee the operation of trains carrying the U.S. Mail. While Funston claimed that he called in troops only to assist the police and fire departments, later critics of his actions would decry that his order to "shoot instantly any person caught looting or committing any serious misdemeanor" was in effect a declaration of martial law. Whatever his intent, by noon the military under Funston's command would reach more than 1,500, and no honest citizen or wharf rat was ready to dispute the authority claimed by a soldier holding a locked and loaded rifle with a fixed bayonet and barking orders at civilians to stop what they were doing.

By twelve o'clock, General Funston was issuing orders from a new location. The approach of the raging fires had forced abandonment of the Phelan Building at eleven o'clock. Since he'd arrived at the building before six o'clock, he had not been in contact with the official whom the people of San Francisco had elected and twice reelected to be their leader.

At about the time General Funston showed up and barked orders at the Phelan Building, Mayor Eugene Schmitz was in his home on Fillmore Street and listening incredulously while an aide, John T. Williams, informed him that the earthquake that had awakened Schmitz a quarter of an hour earlier had not been as insignificant as Schmitz had believed. The mayor exclaimed, "I've got to go to City Hall at once."

Williams answered that City Hall was in ruins. Only the steel skeleton remained of its once elegant, pillared, and stepped rotunda, giving it the appearance of a birdcage. The quake left its graceful dome intact, but it now looked like a derby perched on a hat rack. Its walls resembled the ruins of the ancient Roman Forum or the Parthenon in Athens. Covering four acres and built at a cost of six million dollars, it had taken six years to construct, had rivaled the grandeur of the U.S. Capitol, and had been a magnificent symbol. To the people of the East Coast and of the world, City Hall was the crowning glory of a San Francisco entitled to claim that it was an empire-class city. In April 1906, it was more worthy than ever to call itself America's Golden Gate to the Pacific and the Orient. Yet in a few seconds, according to Williams, City Hall had been laid to waste and much of the city had become an expanse of ruins in an inferno.

Heading as fast as possible in an automobile against a tide of refugees, Mayor Schmitz gazed at the bay. "What a mockery," he said angrily, "to see how calm and placid the waters of the bay are when on shore we have such a disaster."

But what a turn of fate for a man for whom Wednesday, April 18, 1906, was to have been the opening of an investigation of allegations that his city administration had become a cesspool of corruption, misfeasance, malfeasance, and nonfeasance.

Presently, the car encountered Army troops en route to the city from Fort Mason under command of Captain M. L. Walker. Schmitz demanded an explanation. Walker answered that General Funston had called them out.

"I am the mayor," Schmitz retorted indignantly. "The new City Hall is destroyed. I am now going to the Hall of Justice. Report with your company at the Hall of Justice, where you will receive orders what to do."

When the automobile carried Schmitz to see the damage to City Hall, Williams would recall, "It was very obvious that the mayor was deeply grieved when he beheld the way it had been shaken." As the car turned onto Market Street on its way to the Hall of Justice downtown, Schmitz had a full view of the devastation. "This is terrible," he exclaimed, "but thank God I am mayor of a brave people."

Schmitz and his aides arrived at the Hall of Justice on Kearny Street opposite Portsmouth Square at 6:45. The building he found looked little better than City Hall. Assured that it was safe to enter, he grimly greeted Police Chief Jeremiah Dinan and John Dougherty of the Fire Department. When the mayor asked why Fire Chief Dennis Sullivan was not there, he was told that Sullivan had been severely injured in the collapse of the Chief's Quarters and taken to Southern Pacific Hospital. In Sullivan's absence, Schmitz officially declared Dougherty the acting chief of the department.

Because electricity had been cut in the Hall of Justice, the mayor began mapping plans by candlelight in the basement of the building. Dougherty reported that fires had broken out in a large portion of the South of Market area and elsewhere, and that broken water mains left his firemen helpless to control them. He indicated on a city map that fires were raging in the commercial district north of Market Street and coursing west toward Van Ness Avenue. Others were out of control in the Mission District. Strong winds, sometimes at gale force, were driving flames and creating drafts that drew the blazes forward like cyclones. Without water, said the acting chief, the only way to stop the advance was to create firebreaks by employing dynamite to knock down surrounding buildings. To that end, he reported, he'd requested dynamite in the form of powder from stores at the Presidio to supplement three hundreds pounds of dynamite in sticks belonging to the city's Engineering Department.

Police Chief Dinan reported that all six hundred of his policemen would be called to duty for as long as required. Informing Dinan that Army troops from the Presidio were on their way, and that he had ordered their captain to bring them to the Hall of Justice, Schmitz gave his first order of the day. "As soon as they arrive," he said, "send fifty men into the banking district, put ten men on every block on Market Street and a guard for the City Hall. Give these men instructions to be as merciful as possible to the poor, unfortunate refugees, but to shoot to kill everyone found looting. We have no time to waste on thieves."

Inmates of the city jail deemed not dangerous were released with a warning that if they were caught breaking the law they would be shot. Dangerous prisoners were sent to Alcatraz.

Next came an order from the mayor that no one who knew and understood the history of San Francisco ever expected to hear: "Close up every saloon at once."

At the rate the fires had advanced and were continuing to march across the city it was a good bet that police would not find many drinking establishments standing or not burning. Any not reduced to rubble by the earthquake or to ashes would probably have been looted long before any policemen or soldiers showed up to order the place shut.

Also gone or threatened were Barbary Coast bordellos where a man could quaff a drink downstairs before or after going up for whatever tryst he desired or could pay for. When the whorehouses collapsed, the women fled to open spaces to mingle with other refugees. Social class and how someone earned a living suddenly became irrelevant, if only temporarily. For the dazed and terrified seeking safety in wide-open spaces there was no distinction between a Metropolitan Opera diva and a Morton Street prostitute who'd fled from one of Jerome Bassity's parlor houses wearing a sexy Chinese-silk robe.

By mid-morning, the sight of men in uniforms was welcomed, whether they wore the dark-blue police tunics or olive drab breeches with strapped leggings, campaign hats, and russet-colored boots of rifle-toting infantry from the Presidio. Men from the Army and Navy posts on Mare Island who had crossed the bay aboard the *Preble* landed at 10:30 at the foot of Howard Street to help the wounded and dying at Harbor Emergency Hospital.

Because the city's Central Emergency Hospital, located in a portion of the basement of City Hall, had suffered severe fire damage, its staff had evacuated patients directly across the street to the Mechanics Pavilion. An immense, barn-like building between Larkin and Polk Streets, its original purpose was entertainment. Several hours before the earthquake struck, there had been a roller-skating derby. A few days earlier Jack O'Brien had brought prizefight fans to their feet by knocking out Bob Fitzsimmons in the thirteenth round. Through the years, the arena had been used for religious revival meetings, fairs, society balls, and demonstrations of motion pictures. But on the morning of April 18, 1906, a newspaper reporter found its space "filled with dead, dying and injured." He wrote:

> Its vaulted ceiling echoed their cries and moans. Fully 300 persons were treated. Doctors and nurses by the score hurried to the scene and volunteered their much-needed aid. Drugs stores were broken into for medical supplies, and the department stores ransacked for pillows and mattresses for the injured.
>
> The scenes and cries were fearful to behold and hear. The operating rooms were filled all the time. Infants were brought in in their mothers's [*sic*] arms, burned and bleeding. Men and women had been caught by falling walls and horribly mangled, in many cases the broken bones protruding through the flesh.

When fire reached the Pavilion at one o'clock, Dr. Charles Miller, the chief surgeon, ordered everyone out. All kinds of vehicles were commandeered to transport the living and dead to the hospital at the Presidio and to a makeshift open-air hospital in Golden Gate Park.

"Never was there such a scene in San Francisco as there was in Mechanics Pavilion," the reporter wrote, praising the doctors, assistants and nurses. "Their efforts will long be remembered. Young women from the hospitals, graduates in nursing homes, neighbor women and those who drove to the door of the Mechanics Pavilion in their private automobiles, all took a hand in the work. Catholic sisters worked by the side of Salvation Army lasses, and the priests and ministers made their way among the cots, giving the comfort of their cloth."

Red Cross worker O. K. Carr recalled:

Those with mangled bodies and broken or burned limbs begged to be shot to escape being burned alive. Three hundred and fifty in the Pavilion were chloroformed by doctors and nurses and shot by soldiers. It was done as an act of humanity.

I was among the very last to leave the building, and we did not leave a single person to be burned alive. I did not administer chloroform to anyone, nor did I put anyone to death. Only the doctors and nurses handled the drug, and the soldiers did the shooting.

The fire that would eventually attack the Mechanics Pavilion and all buildings in the area of the city known as Hayes Valley got the name "Ham and Eggs Fire." Its start was attributed to a woman who lived on Hayes Street in a house that had been only slightly damaged by the earthquake. Between nine and ten o'clock, she'd decided to cook a breakfast of ham and eggs for her family. Little did she know that the flue of the coal stove had become blocked.

Hot cinders were sent flying, starting a fire that spread from the house to the others on Hayes, Franklin, and Gough Streets until it engulfed not only Mechanics Pavilion, but the St. Nicholas Hotel, the St. Ignatius Church, the ruins of City Hall, and the Hall of Justice.

Ensconced in the basement of the Hall of Justice since 6:45, Mayor Schmitz had made a list of fifty public and private sector leaders and dispatched couriers to locate the men in their homes, places of business, or anywhere else they might be. They were to come to the

Hall of Justice at one o'clock. This was not a request; it was an official summons. Among those summoned were former mayor James D. Phelan, former city attorney Franklin K. Lane, ex-judge C. W. Slack, real estate tycoons Thomas Magee and J. T. Howell, financiers Hartley and Herbert Law, millionaire J. Downey Harvey, Tivoli Opera House manager W. H. Leary, and attorney Garrett W. McEnerney, who'd been expecting to participate that very day in the beginning of hearings on the subject of corruption in Mayor Schmitz's administration.

These men and others became the "Committee of Fifty" and would advise the mayor and provide their prestige and credibility to the handling of the crisis. Although Schmitz's inclusion of men who had been eager to see him prosecuted as a crook appeared to many observers to be a blatant attempt to undermine the corruption investigation, the mayor explained that in choosing them, "I considered neither nationality, creed, nor political affiliation, but picked out the men of the community that I thought were best suited for the task that then confronted them, and seemed by their abilities best equipped to solve the problems and carry into effect the propositions that would come before them."

Also at the meeting were Police Chief Dinan and General Funston, but Schmitz left no doubt that the forces they had commanded to that moment were now taking their orders from the mayor. The first order of business he proposed was a proclamation:

> The Federal Troops, the members of the Regular Police Force and all Special Police Officers have been authorized by me to KILL any and all persons found engaged in Looting or in the Commission of Any Other Crime.
>
> I have directed all the Gas and Electric Lighting Co.'s not to turn on Gas or Electricity until I order them to do so. You may therefore expect the city to remain in darkness for an indefinite time.
>
> I request all citizens to remain at home from darkness until daylight every night until order is restored.

I WARN all Citizens of the danger of fire from Damaged or Destroyed Chimneys, Broken or Leaking Gas Pipes of Fixtures, or any like Cause.

E. E. SCHMITZ, Mayor

With the assent of men described by one historian as "masters of business and captains of industry utterly at a loss and incapable of any initiative in such a terrible emergency," the former professional musician took dictatorial powers with the confidence he'd shown as an orchestra leader.

"He swung his baton and played his new band," wrote historian John Castillo Kennedy, "with as much aplomb as if he had been conducting it for years."

Nowhere in sight at the Hall of Justice on that early Wednesday afternoon was the figure that had provided the libretto for Eugene Schmitz's rise to power. What on April 17 had appeared to be like a Greek tragedy rushing toward a climax of ruin and prison, took a dramatic twist of fate in the form of an earthly upheaval at 5:13 A.M. on April 18.

A newspaper reporter noted, "No time was lost at the meeting, and almost the first words spoken by the Mayor breathed strongly of the grimness of the disaster and its accompaniments."

Schmitz told the committee members that he had secured 2,400 tents and that they were "in process of erection in Jefferson Square, Golden Gate Park and on the Presidio grounds, for the accommodation of the homeless." He also announced that a request had been sent to the state capital that Governor George Pardee immediately send troops of the state militia.

Schmitz was authorized by the committee "to draw checks for any amount for the relief of the suffering." All those present pledged themselves "to make such checks good." Former Mayor Phelan was named chairman of a relief finance committee with full authority to select his associates.

Schmitz ordered a special guard for City Hall to secure vaults in the treasurer's office that contained six million dollars.

Informed by Police Chief Dinan that express men were charging thirty dollars a load to haul goods from stricken homes, the mayor replied, "Tell your men to seize the wagons of all such would-be extortionists, and make use of them for the public good. The question of reccompense will be seen to later."

Schmitz agreed with General Funston that patrol of "the wealthy residence district west of Van Ness Avenue" should be assigned to the Army, "in order to prevent robbery or disorder by the vast throngs being driven thither by the progress of the fire." Accordingly, Funston placed all troops in the city under the command of Colonel Charles Morris of the Artillery Corps. Earlier that morning, he had judged Funston's order to bring troops into the city to be in violation of the U.S. Constitution and a usurpation by a brigadier general of presidential powers, but he was an officer under orders and required to obey them. Now he was in command of a force that he believed was illegal. While General Funston was attending the mayor's meeting at the Hall of Justice, the number of troops in the city exceeded 1,500, with more on the way.

At the outset of the greatest challenge in Funston's distinguished military career, he had sent a telegram to the high command in Washington to report what he'd done and intended to do to cooperate with the civil government. He'd asserted that he trusted the War Department "to authorize any action I may have to take."

Army Chief of Staff General J. Franklin Bell shot back that Funston must "wire details as comprehensively as possible." Then arrived a message from Secretary of War William Howard Taft. He'd sniped, "I wish that you would report to me at once what you have done, the measures you have taken, and under what authority you are acting. Wire as soon as possible."

As this exchange took place, General Funston was operating in the Phelan Building. But at 11:00, he and his staff abandoned headquarters because of fire. He was forced to run the Army by means of couriers who had to carry messages against a tide of panicked refugees in all the streets. At mid-morning, he received a summons from Mayor Schmitz to attend the meeting at the Hall of Justice that began at one o'clock.

Still in session two hours later, the conference of the improvised committee heard that the Ham and Eggs fire was rapidly nearing the Hall of Justice. As evacuation was discussed, the men in the basement heard a blast of dynamite a block away that shook the Hall of Justice and brought glass and cornice work crashing down. Committee member W. H. Leary said, "Your life is too valuable, Mayor, at this dreadful juncture for any unnecessary risk to be taken."

The committee agreed to shift its meeting elsewhere, immediately. Schmitz declared that it would reconvene at the under-construction Fairmont Hotel atop Nob Hill. He reasoned that it did not seem possible that the fire could reach it, but if it did, "it could not do any damage."

Forty minutes before Schmitz ordered his advisors to flee the Hall of Justice, the fire had compelled evacuation of the Postal Telegraph office at the corner of Market and Montgomery. Using the city's only direct link to the rest of the world, the chief operator signaled:

> The city practically ruined by fire. It's within half block of us. The Call building is burned out entirely, the Examiner just fell in a heap. Fire all around in every direction and way out in residence district. Destruction by earthquake something frightful. The City Hall dome stripped and only the framework standing. The St. Ignatius Church and College are burned to the ground. The Emporium is gone, entire building, also the Old Flood Building. Lots of new buildings just recently finished are completely destroyed. They are blowing up standing buildings that are in the path of flames with dynamite. No water. It's awful. There is no communications anywhere and entire phone system is busted. I want to get out of here or be blown up.

37

Moments later, he advised, "I'm packing up the instruments." This was quickly followed by: "Instruments all packed up and I'm ready to run." Then, "Good-bye."

A reporter for the *Chicago American* managed to send a story of everything that a visitor, Helen Dare, had experienced. It began, "No one who has not seen such a disaster that has befallen San Francisco can have any realization of the horror of it, of the pitiful helplessness and inadequacy of human beings thus suddenly cast before the destroying forces of nature."

Four

❀

SPECIAL CORRESPONDENT

❀

WHEN *COLLIER'S* MAGAZINE SENT A telegram to celebrated writer Jack London at his ranch in Sonoma County, hiring him as a special correspondent to report on the earthquake, the author of *The Call of the Wild* and *The Sea Wolf* left immediately. He arrived late in the afternoon on Wednesday. Of the sight from a boat in the middle of the bay he would write, "Not in history has a modern imperial city been so completely destroyed. San Francisco is gone!"

Born John Griffith Chaney in the South of Market section of the city on January 12, 1876, Jack spent much of his youth knocking around the waterfront in Oakland, reading in the public library, and growing more and more eager to explore the rest of the world. His father, William, was an itinerant astrologer and journalist who chose not to marry Jack's mother and deserted her before Jack was born. Eight months later, she married John London, a Civil War veteran who had recently come to San Francisco. Jack did not learn of his true biological father until he was in his twenties. By then Jack had briefly quit school, returned and graduated from Oakland High School, and found after six months at the University of California at Berkeley that college was "not alive enough." He went gold prospecting in Alaska, joined Coxey's Army in a futile march on Washington to protest economic conditions, and worked as a newspaperman. For the Hearst newspapers he'd covered the Russo-Japanese War and gone to Mexico to report a revolution for *Collier's*.

He'd also married twice and used money earned from his bestselling books to buy and expand a ranch in the Valley of the Moon in Sonoma County. Although the earthquake had rattled the property, he did not realize the devastation of his birth city until he got his first view of the conflagration from the boat on a bay that was dead calm. "Not a flicker of wind stirred," he wrote. "Yet from every side wind was pouring in upon the city. East, west, north, and south, strong winds were blowing upon the doomed city. The heated air rising made an enormous suck. Thus did the fire of itself build its own colossal chimney through the atmosphere. Day and night this dead calm continued [on the bay], and yet, near to the flames, the wind was often a gale, so mighty was the suck."

Landing and venturing into a burning city that "crashed and roared into ruin," he found himself amazed that there was no shouting and yelling. "There was no hysteria, no disorder," he reported. He continued:

> I passed Wednesday night in the path of the advancing flames, and in all those terrible hours I saw not one woman who wept, not one man who was excited, not one person who was in the slightest degree panic stricken.
>
> Before the flames, throughout the night, fled tens of thousands of homeless ones. Some were wrapped in blankets. Others carried bundles of bedding and dear household treasures. Sometimes a whole family was harnessed to a carriage or delivery wagon that was weighted down with their possessions. Baby buggies, toy wagons, and go-carts were used as trucks, while every other person was dragging a trunk, yet everybody was gracious. The most perfect courtesy obtained. Never in all San Francisco's history, were her people so kind and courteous as on this night of terror.

At eight o'clock London was in Union Square watching a man offer a thousand dollars for a team of horses that had pulled a cartload of trunks and other material from a hotel to a place thought to be safe. The man in charge refused to part with the horses. Standing nearby was an elderly man leaning on crutches. "Today is my birthday," he said to London. "Last night I was worth thirty thousand dollars. I bought five bottles of wine, some delicate fish and other things for my birthday dinner. Today I have had no dinner, and all I own are these crutches."

London convinced the man of his danger and helped him limp away. "An hour later, from a distance," London recalled, he looked back at the hotel truck and its load of trunks "burning merrily in the middle of the street."

Returning to Union Square five hours later, London remembered that when he'd passed through the first time, the park was packed with refugees. Thousands had gone to sleep on the grass. Some Army tents had been set up, supper was being cooked, and people lined up for free meals. But at half past one in the morning, three sides of Union Square were ablaze. The fourth side, where the St. Francis Hotel stood, appeared to be holding out against the spread of the fire. But within the next hour, the St. Francis ignited, "flaming upward," and the square, "heaped high with mountains of trunks," was deserted. "Troops, refugees, and all," he wrote, "had retreated." It seemed as if every person in San Francisco was struggling to save a trunk.

All night these tens of thousands fled before the flames. Many of them, the poor people from the labor ghetto, had fled all day as well. They had left their homes burdened with possessions. Now and again they lightened up, flinging out upon the street clothing and treasures they had dragged for miles.

They held on longest to their trunks, and over these trunks many a strong man broke his heart that night. The hills of San Francisco are steep, and up these hills, mile after mile, were the trunks dragged. Everywhere were trunks with across them lying their exhausted owners, men and women.

Struggling with their loads, the refugees found themselves confronted by soldiers, most with fixed bayonets. Their orders were to keep people moving.

"These exhausted creatures," London wrote, "stirred by the menace of bayonets, would rise and struggle up the steep pavements, pausing from weakness every five or ten feet. Often, after surmounting a heart-breaking hill, they would find another wall of flame advancing upon them at right angles and be compelled to change anew the line of their retreat. In the end, completely played out, after toiling for a dozen hours like giants, thousands of them were compelled to abandon their trunks."

He further reported, "Here the shopkeepers and soft members of the middle class were at a disadvantage. But the working-men dug holes in vacant lots and backyards and buried their trunks."

In "the very heart of the city" at nine o'clock, London walked through "miles and miles of magnificent buildings and towering skyscrapers," but encountered no fire. Of this richest part of the city, with numerous banks, he observed, "All was in perfect order. The police patrolled the streets. Every building had its watchman at the door."

Returning four hours later, he found everything still intact. There was no fire. And yet there was an ominous difference. A rain of ashes was falling. "The watchmen at the doors were gone," he noted. "There were no firemen, no fire engines, no men fighting with dynamite. The district had been absolutely abandoned. I stood at Kearny and Market, the very innermost heart of San Francisco. Kearny Street was deserted. Half a dozen blocks away it was burning on both sides. The street was a wall of flame. Against this wall of flame, silhouetted sharply, were two United States cavalrymen on their horses. That was all. Not another person was in sight. In the intact heart of the city two troopers sat their horses and watched."

Five

❀

AS GOOD AS A REGIMENT

❀

*A*T 8:40 P.M., BRIGADIER GENERAL Frederick Funston telegraphed the War Department in Washington, D.C. He estimated the death toll at one thousand, and asked that thousands of tents and all available rations be sent for the relief of survivors. That he was able to send a message was the result of heroic work by the Signal Corps.

When the quake began at 5:13 A.M., its San Francisco roster consisted of a captain (Wildman), two sergeants (Binkley and Mosley), a corporal (Deir), and several privates. Funston's first order of the day was sent to Wildman via a courier. Wildman then sent out another messenger in the only U.S. government-owned automobile in San Francisco to the ferry docks at Folsom Street with messages for troops stationed on Alcatraz and Angel islands, ordering them into the city. The courier then motored to the Presidio to notify the officer in charge of Fort Miley of an order from Funston to bring his men into the city to stand guard in the banking district.

By ten o'clock, a telegraph wire was established between the Presidio and the edge of the burning district, and connected to an underwater cable to Oakland. When the fire forced the abandonment of the Postal Telegraph Building at three in the afternoon, this line would be the city's only means of communication with the rest of the world. The man in charge of all outgoing information was a

43

general whose superior officer was out of town to perform a proud father's duty of giving away his daughter at her wedding.

One contemporary historian of the earthquake described General Funston as an "absolute dictator," one who "violated the Constitution and laws of the country at every turn." At one point, U.S. Secretary of War William Howard Taft exclaimed in exasperation to aides, "It would take an act of Congress to relieve him of the responsibility for the violence the army [has done] to the Constitution." So in the dark about events in San Francisco at the outset was President Theodore Roosevelt that he wired Mayor Schmitz, "Hear rumors of great disaster through an earthquake at San Francisco, but know nothing of the real facts. Call upon me for any assistance I can send."

The same historian who termed Funston a dictator went on to praise him for turning "loose the soldiers with broad orders and general instructions to act as their own good sense dictated, and the non-commissioned officers and privates proved their worth. [These army men], supplemented finally by marines and sailors of the fleet, made themselves masters of the situation, and with ruthless but kindly disregard of law and precedent they restored order, carried the homeless to shelter, fed the hungry and portioned out precious water to the people who were clamoring for relief."

General Funston, in taking military command, extended his reach beyond the Army to the naval units in the immediate vicinity of the city. As cited earlier, among the first of these acts was the ordering of the destroyer *Preble* from the naval base at Mare Island to bring doctors to assist at Harbor Hospital. The temporary skipper of the *Preble* was Lieutenant Frederick Freeman. When he received Funston's order, he brought the ship to full boiler power and set off. With her went the fireboat *Leslie* and the tugs *Active* and *Sotomayo*. Upon arrival, Freeman sought out a battalion chief of the fire department and informed him that his ships and men were at his disposal.

"During the fire as witnessed by me," Freeman wrote in an official report, "the men of this party were always willing, and at times when the firemen of the city fire department had to stop in order to look out for their own families, the force under my command, who had no kin to look out for, stuck to their posts until they collapsed."

When the battalion chief was completely exhausted, Freeman took over. In addition to fighting the fire, he and his men had to contend with "a large number of drunken people along the waterfront." His sailors were unarmed, except for two officers who carried revolvers, and in the absence of police Freeman and his crews felt helpless as the crowds "rushed saloon after saloon and looted the stocks."

Freeman wrote in his report, "In my opinion great loss of life resulted from men and women becoming stupefied by liquor and being too tired and exhausted to get out of the way of the fire. During this whole day we needed unarmed men to rescue women and children in the neighborhood of Rincon Hill, the fire having made a clean sweep of this poor residence district in about an hour's time. The most heartrending sights were witnessed in this neighborhood, but with my handful of men we could not do as much for the helpless as we wished. Able-bodied men [civilians] refused to work with the fire department, stating that they would not work for less than forty cents an hour. Men refused to aid old and crippled men and women out of the way of the fire and only thought of themselves."

With no instructions regarding the preservation of order, Freeman heard rumors that the military was in control of the city. He took the report as fact and, in the absence of police, assumed personal command of the waterfront. Worried that soldiers might choose to desert, he ordered that all "stragglers in uniform" be arrested. He was informed that each ferryboat coming in from Oakland brought thousands of sightseers, and commanded the Southern Pacific Company to desist unless General Funston countermanded the order.

Positioned at Pier 8 at the foot of Howard Street, the tugs under Freeman's command assisted the fire department in bringing under control a blaze that would have consumed Folger's Warehouses, the Sailors' Home, and the Mutual Electric Light Company, one of the few remaining power plants in the city.

Soldiers seemed to be everywhere. At almost every street corner, with fixed bayonet and ominous rifle and cartridge belt, infantry, cavalry, and engineers were on sentry duty. If a dapper young cavalry lieutenant appeared in a street, people watched from porches with what one observer called "pathetic anxiety" as he clicked his heels, put down his carbine, made a megaphone of his hands, and announced, "This street is going to be dynamited."

"At the warning of the sentry," the observer continued, "the whole family in each house would rush back through the front door to rescue whatever treasure lay nearest their hearts. They only had four or five minutes. Men would come dragging bureaus and lounges. Often a man would be pulling along the family pride, the woman shoving from behind. Presently, the sentry would shout another warning and the people would scurry away, peeking out from behind safe corners. As if by magic, the streets would be thick with soldiers. The engineers would place the dynamite and they would all hurry out of danger. Bang!"

Just as Jack London had noted, this anonymous observer recalled that "San Francisco in this time of panic and distress was more quiet and orderly than ever before. I saw not a single disturbance of the peace. With it all, the soldiers were polite, and seemed to try in every way to show courtesy and consideration. When they had to order people back, they did it in a quiet and gentlemanly way."

The account continued:

It should be called the "Exodus," for it was a Biblical scene. It was the headlong flight of those who were most terror-stricken to get out of the doomed city. All day long a procession of almost countless thousands was to be seen hurrying with all the possessions they could carry. There were people with bundles, packs, laden express wagons, hacks bulging with plunder, brewery wagons pressed into service, automobiles, push carts, even fire hose wagons. I happened along at a crucial moment. One of the lieutenants whose peculiar and melancholy function seemed to be to pronounce the doom of one section after another, had just sent warning to Nob Hill, the center of fashion in San Francisco.

For hours I had been working my way toward the Oakland ferries. As a last hope, some one told me I might get there by going over these hills and following the line of the water front. I got there after the warning had been given. It was San Francisco's wealthiest and most exclusive society who had to pack and sling their bundles over their shoulders. And they did it with just as good grace and courage as the others. All were making a frantic attempt to hire express men with any kind of vehicle that would move, and most of them were failing.

During the first of the fire, some young society women with very poor taste went autoing around the stricken districts as though it were a circus. They were stopped by a sentry and were made to get out of their car and hand it over to a posse of special officers being hurried to some district in new peril.

As I gained the top of Nob Hill and turned to look back, it was clear why the warning had been given. In one direction, hospitals were burning south of Market Street. In the center distance the big car barns were on fire and roaring with flames. Ordinarily this would have been a sensation of a week. Now it wasn't even considered worth while to send fire engines and nobody stopped to look as they walked by.

The main streets, where the business part of the city had been, were black with an immense throng of people who were walking up and down among the ruins. Looking toward the ferries, I could count nine big skyscrapers, all crowned with fire, outlined in a lurid row against the sky line. The flames were creeping slowly, but with deadly persistence, toward Nob Hill, with several lesser fires blazing in between.

The "Exodus" fled down Van Ness Avenue to the waterfront, along the Barbary Coast and the Embarcadero by way of an enormously long detour in hopes of reaching the ferries. Streets that were blazing on both sides were closed by the military.

"The farther you went along the more conglomerate the throng became," continued this anonymous account. "I was so tired with a long day spent walking about the burning city that it seemed an impossibility that I should keep on. Every step was actual physical pain. Twenty passing cabs, returning from the ferries, I stopped and tried to charter. The drivers, after bigger game, would wave me aside and say 'Nothin' doin'.' One cabby said that he had to hurry out to the other end of the city to rescue his own family who were in danger. Another young autocrat on the cabby's box took a long puff on his cigarette before he replied, 'Fellow, you couldn't hire this hack for a million dollars.' "

Two months after the earthquake and fire, the *Chronicle* published a story about a trio of Army men "recruited from God knows where," who "proved the ability of the American soldier to think and act for himself without any Congress-made officer to bawl drill regulations." It was an account of three infantrymen who'd become separated from their command while trying to save fire apparatus. Organizing a relief expedition, they commandeered wagons and pressed them into service. With "no other authority" than their Jorgensen and Krag rifles, Privates Frank P. McGurty, William Ziegler and Henry Johnson formed wagon trains to transport supplies for refugees at North Beach. They then supervised the building of two "villages" of Army tents that housed 500 and 1,500 people, respectively.

"We didn't have no authority," said McGurty, "but something had to be done, and it seemed to be up to us."

Headlined "SOLDIERS THREE AS GOOD AS A REGIMENT," the *Chronicle* article began: "There isn't any Kipling to chronicle the adventures of these 'Soldiers Three,' but the [characters in the Kipling tale] never had an adventure to compare with what befell their American prototypes, McGurty, Ziegler and Johnson of Company E, Twenty-second United States Infantry, during the San Francisco fire."

It concluded, "The military power of the United States lies in the fact that the American regular soldier can be a machine when a machine is needed, but when a command is so separated that each man acts on his own initiative Mr. Private Soldier uses his brains as well as his eyes, whether his name be McGurty, Ziegler or Johnson, or any other American sounding name."

Not all soldiers lived up to the standards as set by the *Chronicle*. Some demonstrated as great a zeal for looting as civilians. After men in Army uniforms ransacked the Reynolds & Company tobacco store, the firm's lawyer said that this "betrayal of trust by these renegade soldiers is an added aggravation to the crimes of pillage and loot."

A shocked citizen reported witnessing soldiers enter George & Company clothiers and come out, "laden with bundles and boxes of clothing, underwear, overalls, shirts, etc., etc."

Taking to heart Mayor Schmitz's order to "shoot down anyone caught stealing," Army men would summarily execute at least 500 people by bullet or bayonet. A scavenger who was caught pillaging a corpse was hanged from a telephone pole. Another story involved a soldier shooting a man for not obeying an order, only to be told the man was deaf. Other horror stories of soldierly abuse made the rounds. Some were true, but most were false or exaggerated.

Countless times were soldiers on duty on the streets of San Francisco likely to hear a citizen exclaim, "Thank God for the soldiers!"

Six

※

CITY ACROSS THE BAY

※

AYOR FRANK M. MOTT OF OAKLAND believed his city had gotten off comparatively luckily. "The earthquake this morning visited upon our city a great calamity," he said in a proclamation, "yet it is a source of much satisfaction that we were spared from a conflagration and a serious loss of life. The officials of the city have the situation well in hand but I desire to appeal to the people to cooperate with the authorities in maintaining peace and order. As many buildings are in an unsafe condition the public are admonished to keep off the streets, and particularly warned against congregating in groups."

Oakland's history, like San Francisco's, was that of early Spanish colonization of land that had belonged to Indians. These first occupants had used it as a place for ritual purification rites around fires in huts called Temescals. White settlers called the area "Ensinal de Temescal," which means "the oak grove by the sweathouse." Again, like San Francisco, Oakland was in Mexican hands until America's takeover in 1848. Among the "Forty-Niners" who came seeking treasure were men who discerned a profit to be made in what could be grown on the land. When an easterner named Moses Chase joined three brothers by the name of Patten to farm 460 acres, they called it "Rancho San Antonio." But with San Francisco mushrooming in the 1850s and having an insatiable need for lumber, the Pattens went into the timber business. They harvested redwoods, and soon had more than four hundred men at work in several mills.

When a portion of Rancho San Antonio was put up for sale, another easterner, Horace W. Charpentier, acquired a sizeable chunk by methods that the locals deemed "slick," and quite likely illegal. He incorporated a town with a name inspired by its abundant oak trees. He then anointed himself Mayor of Oakland. The first ferry service between the sister bay cities began operating in 1850. The railroad arrived in 1863. Thirty years later, Oakland's population stood at 50,000. Because it was overshadowed by its neighbor in the way that New York City's sister city across the East River was, it gained the nickname "the Brooklyn of San Francisco." When the earthquake and fire of April 18, 1906, caused citizens of the city of Saint Francis to seek refuge, they rushed to the Ferry Building and swarmed toward the city of oaks. More than 150,000 would arrive and over 65,000 would stay.

One refugee claimed that Oakland was "the star of hope to which all eyes were turning." It was "such a little distance across a narrow stretch of water, and yet such a great way for the crippled, the fatigued, the exhausted, the footsore, and the heartsick; a stretch of continents for the mother trying to carry her dying child to safety, the wife kneeling in the streets alongside her injured and suffering husband; the husband upon whose shoulders were more years than strength could combat and whose gray head was bowed over another lying helpless there on the ground and into whose eyes he did not dare look lest the fear in his heart would prove well founded."

A newspaper account of the stream of humanity noted, "Thousands of refugees, rendered homeless by the terrible calamity which has overtaken San Francisco, have come to this city to escape from the terrors across the bay. On learning of this the Realty Syndicate at once offered Idora Park for the use of those left without shelter by the earthquake. The offer has been gratefully accepted by the Police and Fire Commissioners, and two hundred cots have been placed in the theater for use of the refugees. Relief stations have also been established at the

City Hall, and at the various public parks throughout the city."

Worried that Oakland might also become an inferno, Fire Chief N. A. Ball warned the populace, "Build no fires in coal stoves, grates or fire places until the interior of the chimneys has been inspected, cleaned out and put in repair. In many places where the chimneys appear to be all right, they may have cracks in the interior or may have stopped up with refuse, which might cause a blind fire." Mayor Mott's similar warning added, "Those who have not either gas or oil stoves are advised that danger may be avoided by moving their stoves out of doors."

"It is at present impossible to estimate the amount of damage to property in this city," said a newspaper the next day, "owing to the fact that practically no inspection has been made of the buildings, except by Fire Warden George McDonald, and this only for the purpose of condemning those which are unsafe and must be torn down. Many of the structures which from the outside show little apparent damage, on closer examination prove to have been so badly twisted and racked by the shock that it is feared they will have to be torn down."

The only known deaths from collapsing walls were five unlucky people caught inside a theater when it caved in. Among the most obvious structural victims of the quake was a pair of smokestacks of a gas works. They'd crashed through the plant's roof, crushing the boiler, and killing a man who stoked the fire. Across from Lake Merritt, a saltwater body a few blocks away from the waterfront, the Twelfth Street dam sunk eighteen inches from the force of the earthquake.

Still standing and open for business was a place familiar to Jack London. Built in 1883 by J. H. Heinhold from the timbers of an old whaling ship, the "First and Last Chance Saloon" got its name because it afforded anyone coming from and going to "dry" Alameda a chance to "get liquored up." The saloon provided seventeen-year-old London with a place to study and write, thanks to its sympathetic owner. When London needed tuition money to attend the University of California at Berkeley, Heinhold lent him three hundred dollars. London repaid the generosity by frequently mentioning the First and Last Chance Saloon in his novels. This resulted in a fame that clings to the saloon to this day as it stands on land that is now called Jack London Square.

The university that would move to Berkeley in 1865 was originally opened as a preparatory school in Oakland in 1855. Although many structures in the city suffered severe damage in the quake, including the city hall, the university escaped, as one writer put it, "as by a miracle." The same could not be said of Stanford University in Palo Alto. Among the university's devastated landmarks was Memorial Chapel. Extolled as "the finest church building in the Western Hemisphere," its exterior and interior walls were covered "with the most beautiful and elaborate carvings, mosaics, stained glass windows and statuary." It was shattered from steeple to foundation.

The Memorial Arch, said to be the second highest in the world, looked as if it had been hit by cannon fire. Standing just inside the main gate, it was a hundred feet high, ninety feet wide and thirty-four feet deep. Beneath the arch stood a sculpture of the Stanford family—father, mother, and son. Elsewhere on campus, a white marble statue in the memory of Mrs. Leland Stanford's late brother, called "Angel of Grief," was in chunks. In the city of Palo Alto, the low-lying area on the edge of the bay was swept by a tidal wave.

At Santa Rosa, the seat of government in Jack London's adopted Sonoma County, almost all government, business, and residential buildings were destroyed or so severely damaged that they were beyond saving. Left in ruins by the quake and subsequent fires were the courthouse, the Hall of Records, the Occidental and Santa Rosa theaters, a new Masonic Temple, a business block housing the Odd Fellows Hall, and all the banks. Only the depot of the California Northwestern Railroad and a row of grocery and clothing stores remained reasonably intact. As in San Francisco, a company of state militia and marines from Mare Island imposed public order.

Farther south in San Jose, famed as "one of the prettiest cities in California," business structures and churches were destroyed by the quake and fires. In nearby Agnew, the Agnews Insane Asylum collapsed, killing more than two hundred patients. About one hundred students from Santa Clara College broke into scores of padded cells to rescue the others.

The inland agricultural town of Salinas lost all of its major buildings. A landslide on Loma Prieta Mountain buried nine men alive in cabins at the Hinckley Creek mill of the Loma Prieta Lumber Company. Buildings tumbled in Watsonville, Collinsville, Woodlands, Tomales, Stockton, Heraldburg, Cloverdale, Hopeland, Brawley, Fort Bragg, Tajaro, and Ukiah. Between the towns of Castroville and Monterey, reported J. E. Rainey, along railroad tracks and in the fields, "mud geysers have been excited into action, spouting a boiling hot, bluish, shale-colored mud to a height of from ten to twelve feet."

Walls cracked and chimneys fell at San Quentin State Prison, compelling the warden to release screaming, terrified prisoners from cells and herd them into the yard while armed guards looked down nervously from high, thick outer walls.

A contemporary account of this widespread devastation calculated these property losses:

Oakland	$500,000
Alameda	$400,000
San Jose	$3,000,000
Agnew	$400,000
Palo Alto	$4,000,000
Napa	$250,000
Salinas	$2,000,000
Hollister	$200,000
Vallejo	$40,000
Sacramento	$25,000
Redwood City	$30,000
Santa Rosa	$800,000
Watsonville	$70,000
Monterey	$25,000
Santa Cruz	$150,000

Property losses in San Francisco were estimated at $400 million, of which one-fifth ($80 million) was attributed to the earthquake itself. An official U.S. Army report put the death tolls at 498 in San Francisco, 64 in Santa Rosa, and 102 in and near San Jose. The death toll was later estimated, directly and indirectly, at more than 3,000. Those left homeless were estimated to be 225,000. In an area of four square miles, the quake and fire destroyed 24,671 wooden buildings and 3,168 buildings of brick and masonry (total: 28,188).

But late on the night of April 18, 1906, as Jack London prowled the ruined streets of the city of his birth and surveyed the unfolding calamity, he decided that an "enumeration of the buildings destroyed would be a directory of San Francisco." Recounting the deeds of heroism, he would write for *Collier's*, "would stock a library." He predicted, "An enumeration of the dead will never be made. All vestiges of them were destroyed by the flames. The number of victims of the earthquake will never be known."

At quarter past five on Thursday morning, twenty-four hours after the first jolt of the earthquake, he sat on the steps of a small residence on Nob Hill. All about him were the palaces of the "nabob pioneers" of 1849. To the east and south, resembling right angles, two mighty walls of flame were marching up the hill. Troops began to fall back, driving refugees before them. From all sides came the horrible sound of roaring flames, crashing walls, and dynamite exploding.

Seven

THE DEMON

*W*ORRIED THAT BLOWING UP PRIVATE property might result in lawsuits against the city, Mayor Eugene Schmitz sought a legal opinion. The judge, quoting a ruling made during a fire in 1849, informed him that the right to destroy property "to prevent the spread of a conflagration" had been traced to the highest law of necessity and the rights of man, "independent of society or civil government."

Dynamiting of buildings around the U.S. Mint at Fifth and Mission Streets began at 2:30 P.M. on Wednesday. Disagreements on how and where to blast were almost as explosive. Schmitz advocated blowing up buildings close to the fires. General Funston argued that blasting houses near the fire would result in flying splintered wood that would become kindling. He favored creating a wide swath of demolition far ahead that would be too wide for the flames to cross. In the end, Schmitz's method prevailed.

A newspaper reporter observed, "During the day a blast could be heard in any section at intervals of only a few minutes, and buildings not destroyed by fire were blown to atoms." But gaps created drafts, which drew the flames ahead. "Men worked like fiends," the reporter said, "to combat the laughing, roaring, onrushing demon."

At eight o'clock on Wednesday evening, Schmitz was still confident that a large part of downtown could be saved, and that the fire could be prevented from climbing Nob Hill. He called for making a stand at Powell Street. The inviting feature of the street that rose from Market Street to the crest of Nob Hill was that it bordered one side of Union Square. The large park, along with a few surrounding vacant lots, presented a firebreak that would serve the purpose of dynamiting. Firefighters converged at nine o'clock to make their stand along Powell between Sutter and Pine and did so with bravery, but with little hope and even less water. Shortly after midnight, recalled one horrified witness, the streets forming the square were under attack, fueled by a strong westerly wind.

"On three sides ringed with sheets of flame rose the Dewey Memorial in the midst of Union Square," noted another account. "[The figure of] Victory tiptoeing on the apex of the column glowed red, [reflecting] flames. It was as if the goddess of battle had suddenly become apostate and a fiend linked in sympathy with the devils of the blaze."

Smoke eddied from windows of great dry goods stores and "streamed flamboyantly like a poppy-colored silk that jumped skyward in curling, snapping breadths, a fearful heraldry of the pomp of destruction." From copper minarets of the Hebrew Synagogue shot "tiny green" flames that "grew quickly larger, and as the heat increased in intensity there shone from the two great bulbs of metal sheathing an iridescence that blinded like a sight into a blast furnace. With a roar the minarets exploded almost simultaneously, and the sparks shot up to mingle with the dulled stars overhead." The Union League and Pacific Union clubs were next. Then the flames swept the Bohemian, Pacific, Union, and Family clubs and the St. Francis Hotel.

Also obliterated were huge retail stores along Post Street; St. Luke's Church, the biggest Episcopal Church on the Pacific Coast; and the Hopkins Art Institute. As the fire neared the repository of priceless treasures, an infantry lieutenant drew his pistol and conscripted every man within shouting distance to help carry out paintings and sculptures and to place them on the broad lawn of the adjacent Stanford mansion. The rescue would be a brief one; the shift of the wind directed the flames from the waterfront on the north of Market Street toward Nob Hill and its majestic palaces, owned by the richest families in the city.

It was here at the first light of dawn on Thursday that Jack London stirred after a few fruitless hours of trying to sleep. He found "a sickly light." The sun broke briefly through "the smoke-pall, blood-red, and showing quarter its usual size. The smoke-pall itself, viewed from beneath, was a rose color that pulsed and fluttered with lavender shades." Then it turned to mauve, yellow, and dun. "And so dawned the second day," he wrote, "on stricken San Francisco."

A few hours earlier, Lieutenant Frederick Freeman had toured the waterfront aboard the tug *Leslie*. He found the area "apparently safe for the time being," but saw that the fire was on its way toward Nob Hill. Of this dramatic turn, historian Dan Kurzman wrote elegantly in his book *Disaster!*, "The people atop Nob Hill–who had earlier been captivated by the sight of the less affluent areas in the distance vanishing in an ocean of flame–suddenly had a change of heart. The mindless monster, unable to distinguish between the rich and the rabble, the patrician and the plebeian, was now threatening to devour *them*! Their magnificent San Francisco, built by their ancestors on a foundation of gold, was now to go the way of the shanties."

On the brink of Nob Hill at the southwest corner of Powell and California streets was the mansion built by Leland Stanford. A transplanted easterner who was born in 1824 in Watervliet, New York, he'd been a lawyer in Albany and Wisconsin. When his offices burned out in 1852, he migrated to California and went into retail merchandising with his younger brothers. Drawn into politics as a Republican, he'd failed in bids for state treasurer and governor, but benefited from a split in the Democratic Party and was elected governor in 1861. During his term, he joined Collis Huntington, Charles Crocker, and Mark Hopkins in promoting the construction of the Central Pacific

Railroad. Known as the "Big Four," they next developed the Southern Pacific Railroad. Stanford, being opportunistic and ambitious, was elected to the U.S. Senate in 1885 and held the seat until his death in 1893. Fabulously rich, he founded Stanford University and named it after his son and namesake, who'd died in 1884. When his widow died in Honolulu, Hawaii, about a year before the earthquake, the Nob Hill mansion was passed to the university.

Across from Stanford's house was the home of his late partner, Mark Hopkins. Nearby were those of Crocker and mining multimillionaire James Flood, whose huge brownstone mansion cost a million dollars. Opposite the Stanford and Hopkins residences was the Fairmont Hotel. Not yet finished after two years of work, it occupied land owned by Flood; Nevada mining tycoons John W. Mackay and James O'Brien; and the late James Fair, hence the hotel's name. In a retrospective stroke of unfortunate timing some months before the quake, the hotel was traded by Fair's daughter, Theresa (Mrs. Herman Oelrichs), for the Rialto and Crosby buildings, both of which were destroyed, while the hotel would remain upright, but burned out.

It was to the Fairmont Hotel that Mayor Schmitz had adjourned the initial meeting of his emergency committee from the Hall of Justice on Wednesday afternoon. Back on Nob Hill on Thursday morning as the fire advanced toward its summit, he supervised firemen, soldiers, and others carrying countless paintings from doomed houses to lawns and gardens with hopes that they'd be spared from the approaching inferno. Most were not, although a few were rescued by a quick-thinking professor who hacked them out of their wooden frames, rolled up the precious canvases and whisked them away. But there would be no saving the stately mansions. Gone up in flames along with the palaces of the Big Four would be the Spreckles Mansion, financed by a sugar fortune, along with the Spreckles Building on Market Street, home to the *Call*.

Now that the fire had climbed Nob Hill, Mayor Schmitz's fear was that it would sweep down the other side and envelop an area of frame dwellings known as the Western Addition, and roar onward to devour thousands of residences in the Richmond District. Conferring with Police Chief Dinan, Schmitz recognized that the only hope of stopping the advance lay in the breadth of Van Ness Avenue. It was the city's widest thoroughfare at ninety feet across. To stem the tide, every fire engine was summoned, along with police, Funston's soldiers, field artillery units commanded by Colonel Charles Morris, and squads of dynamiters.

The plan called for dynamiting structures on the east side of Van Ness for twenty blocks between the bay and Golden Gate Avenue. The fire department would pump water from the bay and hose down buildings on the west side of the avenue. Soldiers spread out, ordering everyone in houses and businesses to evacuate. Almost immediately, it was clear that the dynamite supply was insufficient, and that efforts by Funston's troops to bring more by boat from military and naval posts were unlikely to succeed in time to stop the advance of the fire.

As it neared the wide avenue, wind carried sparks and embers forward and onto rooftops. When some of them landed on the steeple of St. Mary's Cathedral at 1001 Van Ness Avenue, Father Charles Ramm and other priests scurried into action. While some witnesses credit them with saving the venerable church, an account published in the *Call* cited the efforts of a young fireman, James Lang. The newspaper said that he'd climbed to the top of the tower with an ax strapped to his body to "cut away the blazing woodwork" and save the building.

"A thousand glasses [binoculars] were held upon the brave man as he stood high up above the street cutting away the blazing woodwork," said the article. "He stood there for two hours. When he finally left his post, after the danger to the cathedral had passed, he collapsed from physical and nervous exhaustion."

Not so lucky along Van Ness Avenue were the St. Ignatius Catholic Church, occupying an entire block; St. Bridget's at Van Ness and Broadway, wrecked by the quake; and the St. Luke's

Episcopal Church at Van Ness and Clay, devastated by the quake and then burned out. Also left in ruins were the Temple Emanu-El at Union Square; the Grace Church (Episcopal) at Stockton and California; and the Church of the Holy Cross on Eddy Street between Scott and Devisadero.

A telegraph operator in Oakland tapped out to a receiver in New York City, "The roar of dynamite from the other side of the harbor is almost deafening at times. They are attempting to blast out pathways in the city blocks wherever the fire threatens, in order to check its spread. San Francisco is at times enveloped in smoke, and when it lifts we can see the flames of burning buildings and occasionally the timbers flying from dynamite explosions. Almost all activity except that of dynamiting appears to have ceased."

A guest who had fled from the Palace Hotel on Wednesday to the haven across the water reported, "From Oakland the scene across the bay was terrible. The city was all in flames. At intervals of a few moments there would be tremendous explosions as dynamite or gun cannon [cloth bundles stuffed with gun powder and ignited] was exploded in the buildings that stood in the way of the fire. Tongues of flame hundreds of feet long swept the skies."

Physician Ernest W. Fleming wrote, "The air was filled with the roar of explosions. They were dynamiting great blocks. Sailors were training guns to rake rows of residences."

Resigned to the fact that his splendid home on Van Ness Avenue was fated to be reduced to rubble, but confident that he was wealthy enough to rebuild it, Fulton G. Berry greeted the dynamiters by exclaiming, "Blow her to blazes, boys!"

Wine connoisseur Gordon Blanding invited dynamiters into his cellar to taste the rarest of his vintages before they set the charges.

Mrs. John T. Merrill had opened her beloved house to refugees who'd fled up the hill. Ordered to decamp within half an hour, she told her guests, "I do not want anybody to leave until you have all had some tea and toast." When they had, she instructed servants to put the silver service, crystal, and other treasures into a safe that its maker had guaranteed to be fireproof. It was, but Mrs. Merrill would find its contents, except a cheap watch, melted into a large clump.

"The flames took all there was to take, after the earthquake had given us a mighty shake," said a witness to the devastation, "as if to remind millionaires of their puniness."

Eight

✿

END OF THE WORLD

✿

THROUGH BILLOWS OF SMOKE, JACK London observed a city that reminded him of the crater of a volcano. He wrote that as men and women emerged to creep warily under the shadows of tottering walls, it was like meeting a "handful of survivors after the day of the end of the world."

On Mission Street, he found corpses of a dozen steers in a neat row. Lying "just as they had been struck down by the flying ruins of the earthquake," they had been roasted by the fire. "The human dead," he noted, "had been carried away before the fire came."

"Shut off from the outside world," a contemporary historian wrote in apocalyptic tones, the city was "at once a bleeding, crying wilderness of fear, horror and death" in which "nearly four hundred thousand people awoke to see the result of a century of labor and genius crumble to dust and ashes as though touched by the magic wand of the Demon of Destruction." Into this "groaning, tossing, tumbling chaos" rushed "a half naked and wholly crazed throng of humanity, praying, cursing, weeping, begging and denying." They were "the children of men helpless in the presence of the forces of a Nature they thought they'd made their slaves."

By five o'clock on Wednesday afternoon, twelve hours after the earth began shaking, more than fifty corpses had been buried by police in Portsmouth Square. The city morgue and a makeshift repository for bodies at the police firing range were simply unable to hold more. The living, terrified and walking wounded, flooded to Union Square, the Presidio, Jefferson Square Park, and the largest public space–Golden Gate Park.

Three-quarters-of-a-mile wide, covering more than a thousand acres, and stretching three miles westward to the Pacific Ocean, Golden Gate Park was laid out with eucalyptus, Monterey cypress, and pine trees and adorned with monuments of President James Garfield, Civil War hero Charles Halleck, and Francis Scott Key. It featured a conservatory, a children's playground, Stow Lake for rowing, a Dutch windmill, a Japanese tea garden, a Mexican garden, a small herd of roaming buffalo, a museum with Egyptian architecture, the Spreckles bandstand, a merry-go-round, gravel footpaths, and breathtaking views of ships plying the Golden Gate. The quake did little harm to the museum and bandstand, but it had caused serious damage to the chief playground feature, a sandstone structure known as Sharon Hall, which contained a large lunchroom.

Suddenly converted to an outdoor hospital after the evacuation of the city's emergency room and abandonment of the makeshift medical facility in the Mechanics Pavilion, the park quickly teemed with refugees from all sections of the smashed and burning city. The earliest to arrive claimed the benches in front of the bandstand. All others found rest on whatever piece of lawn they could find. Lost or orphaned children were taken to a section set aside by soldiers.

A visitor from Los Angeles, Dr. Ernest W. Fleming, had escaped his collapsing hotel and wandered aimlessly through the city until he reached the park at dusk on Wednesday. "But it was a weird twilight," he recalled. "The glare from the burning city threw a kind of red flame and shadow about us. It seemed uncanny; the figures about us moved like ghosts. The wind and fog blew chill from the ocean, and we walked to keep warm. Thousands were walking about, too, but there was no disturbance. Families trudged [but] there was no hurry. All appeared to have time to spare. Thousands were moving with us. As the night wore on the crowd grew. Near daylight the soldiers came to the park. They were still moving in front of the fire."

Secretary of War William Howard Taft ordered that the Army take steps to rush material assistance to San Francisco. The chief of staff sent a telegram to the commanding general of the Department of Columbia, Vancouver Barracks, in Washington State. It directed that 200,000 rations be sent "without delay" to the Army Depot Commissary at San Francisco, along with "all available hospital, wall, and conical tents to depot quartermaster, by quickest practicable route either by water or rail." The message continued, "All railroad and telegraph facilities surrounding San Francisco reported badly damaged and demoralized. Have an officer accompany these stores with view to seeing that they are forwarded and delivered as promptly as possible; and instruct him to keep in touch, by wire, with General Funston when practicable."

Army headquarters in Washington, D.C, also directed that hospital and barracks-type tents be sent to the city from Forts Douglas, Logan, Snelling, and Sheridan and the Presidio of Monterey. More tents and other materials were ordered from San Antonio, Texas. At 4:55 A.M., Funston was informed that every tent the Army had would soon be en route to San Francisco.

As dawn broke on Thursday, the brigadier general had been awake for more than twenty-four hours. According to one witness, the de facto dictator of San Francisco had been acting "not from his office," but "plowing around the most perilous streets soaked to the skin." In command of soldiers and a small armada consisting of U.S. Army and Navy boats, tugs, and ships of the California Naval Militia, he issued an order early on Thursday morning to Lieutenant Freeman to have his men seize the tug *Priscilla* and take it to Pinole Point to obtain dynamite. Freeman was authorized to "seize any ship on the waterfront."

One of the busiest of Funston's officers, Freeman found himself not only commandeering boats, but taking charge of dynamite crews and leading fire fighters to save the waterfront. At one point, a hose from the pumping boat *Leslie* stretched five hundred feet down Montgomery Street, from Broadway to New Montgomery Avenue. Running eleven blocks, it was the longest distance that any salt water was carried. It enabled firemen to spray to a height of two-and-a-half stories from the street. From hoses on rooftops of four-story buildings, they were able to save the Bank of Italy, the Appraisers' Building, and Hotaling and Company, a liquor wholesaler.

Poet Charles K. Field would extol the latter rescue with an amusing question in verse that was a challenge to clerics who claimed that the earthquake and fire was a divine punishment for decades of San Francisco's scarlet sins:

> If as some say, God spanked the town
> For being over frisky,
> Why did He burn the churches down
> And save Hotaling's Whiskey?

The officials of Hotaling's Whiskey were delighted, and rewarded the fire fighters and Freeman's men with their product.

With what appeared to be an unintentional joke, Freeman wrote in his official report, "An entirely different spirit seemed to pervade people in this section of the city, as every aid was offered the fire fighters by the citizens [compared to those elsewhere who refused to fight the fires unless they were paid]." As to his own men, he continued, "The men of my command at this point showed the greatest daring and perseverance, going to the tops of buildings and extinguishing fires in cornices and windows, going through large buildings before the fire reached them and tearing down all inflammable material, such as curtains, awnings, etc., and I have no doubt that this section of the city was saved entirely by their efforts."

The contents of refrigerator cars belonging to the meat packing firm Armor & Company, standing on tracks at the wharves, were unable to be saved. But it was not the fire that did them in. "When it became evident that these could not be saved," noted a quake historian, "a flock of 'wharf rats' and hoodlums were permitted to go in and take everything they wanted. A wild scramble ensued, the men and boys fighting desperately for the food."

In an official report to the Navy dated April 30, 1906, Freeman proudly and rightly wrote:

> In summing up the work done by the Mare Island fire tugs I particularly lay claim to the work done in saving the waterfront from Howard Street to the Pacific Mail Docks, the Southern Pacific freight sheds, and that section of the city; the Folsom warehouses and the Mutual Electric Light Company's plant on Spear and Folsom Street and on the north by Jackson Street, including the Appraisers' Building, the Hotaling and Company, the Bank of Italy, which is far from the waterfront; and the saving of the large warehouses in the lee of Telegraph Hill, including Gibraltar Warehouses, the Haslett Warehouse No. 1, the Italian-Swiss Colony Warehouses, etc.; and the stopping of the fire abreast Lombard Street wharf, thereby preventing the fire from sweeping the waterfront and stopping all traffic, which at this time would have been a terrible calamity.

Immediately following the first shock on Wednesday morning, hundreds of displaced and terrified residents of downtown homes and hotel guests had poured into the streets in a rush to the ferry slips with the intent of escaping to Oakland.

In San Francisco on business, Egbert H. Gold, the president of the Chicago Car Heating Company, had been thrown out of bed and onto the floor of his room on the seventh floor of the Palace Hotel. Hurrying to the waterfront, he discovered people "by the thousands and seemingly devoid of reason" crowded around the ferry station. He reported, "At the iron gates they clawed with their hands as so many maniacs. They sought to break the bars, and, failing in that, turned upon each other. Fighting my way to the gate like the others, the thought came to my mind of what rats in a trap were. Had I not been a strong man I should certainly have been killed. When the ferry drew up to the slip, and the gates were thrown open, the rush to safety was tremendous. The people flowed through the passage-way like a mountain torrent that, meeting rocks in its path dashes over them. Those who fell saved themselves as best they could."

Frederick H. Collins, co-owner of Koening and Collins Cloaks and Suits, purveyors of ladies' fashions and millinery, recalled, "In all the misery there are the usual tearfully funny things—people cross[ed on ferry boats] that dreadful morning in nightgowns and barefoot and many ran with the crazies and things they had saved. One woman carried a bird and one shoe. Another a few flat irons. One poor Chinaman crossed the bay with a stick of firewood wrapped up, and some ran with an 'enlarged picture' of someone of the family as a child. Old women and men were seen dragging chairs loaded with things in the way of clothing and blankets, pulled by a little rope over their backs."

Forced to spend Wednesday night "on the hard ground in the open" of Union Square and with arms and legs aching "from so rough a bed," Enrico Caruso was relieved that his valet had suc-ceeded "in getting a man with a cart" who offered "for a certain sum" to take them to the Oakland Ferry. "We pile the luggage into the cart and climb in after it, and the man whips up his horse and we start," Caruso wrote. "We pass terrible scenes on the way: buildings in ruins, and everywhere there seems to be smoke and dust. The driver seems in no hurry, which makes me impatient at times, for I am longing to return to New York, where I know I will find a ship to take me to my beautiful Italy and my little boys. When we arrive in Oakland we find a train there which is just about to start, and the officials are very po-lite, take charge of my luggage, and tell me to get on board, which I am very glad to do."

Caruso found the trip to New York "very long and tedious." He explained that he slept "very little, for I can still feel the terrible rock-ing which made me sick." Writing in the July 1906 issue of *The Theater* magazine of all that he'd been through, he said, "Even now I can only sleep an hour at a time, for the experience was a terrible one."

He never returned to San Francisco.

This would not be true of John Barrymore. Whether returning to tread the stages of its rebuilt and new theaters or as a movie star on excursions from Hollywood, he would be indebted to the city—and the earthquake—for providing him experiences with which to regale his friends for the rest of his life. In addition to the drama of having been rudely awakened by the quake, he could spin a tale of looking down the barrel of a soldier's gun as houses along Van Ness Avenue were being dynamited.

Encountering a friend who couldn't find the key to the door of his home, Barrymore picked up a rock and smashed a window. The noise resulted in the appearance of a soldier with "the biggest-looking gun" Barrymore had ever seen. "Fortunately," he told friends many times through the years, "the man behind the gun asked questions before he shot."

Having explained his way out of danger, and with the friend's treasures carried from the doomed residence, Barrymore made his way to the home of other acquaintances in Burlingame, expecting and hoping that his theatrical troupe was well on the way to Australia. Concerned that his family back East would learn that he was not among the group and fear that he was dead, he bicycled back to San Francisco with the intention of going on to Oakland to send them a telegram. The plan went awry when soldiers stopped him to demand that he assist them in clearing rubble. Learning that their detainee was a famous actor, the soldiers put him in charge of a group of laborers.

"I knew so little about work," he pointed out in relating the episode, "that it was difficult for me to become a good executive."

Delayed about eight hours, he arrived in Oakland and found his friend Ashton Stevens. He told Barrymore he had "good news." The actor had not missed the boat to Australia. It was scheduled to sail from Vancouver in three days. When Barrymore's explanatory telegram got to his sister, Ethel, she read it to their uncle, the esteemed actor John Drew, and wondered if John might be pulling their leg.

"I believe every word of it," said Drew. "It took a convulsion of nature to make him get up and the United States Army to make him go to work."

Nine

❀

GET THE STORY

❀

T 6:45 P.M. ON THURSDAY, APRIL 19, 1906, on the other side of the continent, the publisher of the San Francisco *Examiner* and two New York newspapers was in such a snit over a report from the West Coast that the Army was keeping his people from sending stories on the quake that he shot off a telegram to Secretary of War William Howard Taft:

> INFORMED BY TELEGRAPH COMPANIES THAT WIRES ARE IN OPERATION BUT TRANSMISSION NEWS FORBIDDEN BY MILITARY CENSORSHIP. MUST PROTEST AS THOUSANDS OF THE FRIENDS OF STRICKEN PEOPLE ARE EAGERLY AWAITING NEWS AND DELAY IS CAUSING THEM GREAT DISTRESS.
> W. R. HEARST,
> EDITOR, N.Y. AMERICAN AND JOURNAL

Taft responded that Hearst's information was incorrect, noting that he had "received a dispatch from General Funston this morning saying that he is not interfering with the sending of any dispatches." He continued, "[Funston] says, however, that the confusion is so great that it is impossible now to locate individuals for the delivery of dispatches, or for the giving of information in respect to them."

General Funston certainly had more on his mind than the problems faced by reporters in sending out stories through a telegraph system that had been hastily patched together following the evacuation of the Postal Telegraph Office at three o'clock on Wednesday afternoon. To open a line to a Western Union office in Oakland, men of the Army Signal Corps rushed into the city from the Presidio and established a post at the Ferry Building. Using wire cut from electric lines that had been downed by the quake, they rigged a connection to Fort Mason and hooked up a link to the cable that ran on the bottom of the bay to Oakland with the hope that lines from there to the rest of the country were still in service.

As the Signal Corps struggled with wires in San Francisco, Harry Jeffs, the wire chief of Western Union Telegraph Company in Oakland, scurried to find out how much, if any, of his system was operating. Beginning his checks at the point where the cross-bay cable emerged from the water, he found that the connection to the Ferry Building in San Francisco was functioning, but that it was dead beyond that point. His next task was to check his own lines from the water's edge inland. This meant climbing each telegraph pole and testing its connection by sending a signal to the Western Union office in Sacramento. After numerous disappointments, he finally received a response. At 8:30 on Wednesday morning, with a tenuous hold atop a thirty-foot pole, he transmitted a report of the earthquake. On Thursday morning, repairs to the Oakland pier breaks resulted in three lines being opened. This operation was headquartered in a four-room, waterfront cottage graciously provided by the woman who called it her home. On the San Francisco end, the Western Union Company functioned from a hut on a pier.

Relayed from Sacramento to Los Angeles, Salt Lake City, and Denver, the news flashed across the country and around the world to appear in huge, shocking newspaper headlines and vividly written stories. In New York, the *Times* had a three-tier banner:

OVER 500 DEAD, $200,000,000 LOST IN
SAN FRANCISCO EARTHQUAKE
Nearly Half the City in Ruins and 50,000 Are Homeless
Water Supply Fails and Dynamite is Used in Vain

Devoting the entire front page and vast space inside to details of the earthquake's damage and the out-of-control fire, the paper termed it a "disaster that staggers comprehension and in point of terror and damage is unprecedented on the coast and has not yet reached its culmination."

Page one featured a drawing of the tracing made by the seismograph needle in State Geologist John M. Clarke's office at the State Museum in Albany. A graph of violent up-and-down movements by a recording pen represented "the vibration of the north and south pendulum in a seismograph during the time of the most intense activity." The graph showed that the time of the tremor's transit across the continent was nineteen minutes.

The effect of the quake was felt on the stock exchange on Wall Street. Shares were heavily liquidated in the United Railways Company of San Francisco, operators of the transit system. By day's end, a share's value was 27, a net loss of 15 points.

Another New York paper, the *Sun*, reported, "The greatest earthquake disaster in the history of the United States visited San Francisco early yesterday. A great part of the business and tenement district was shaken down, and this was followed by fire which is still burning and which has covered most of the affected area."

The lengthy, detailed, and often sensational and racist account of the devastation, fires, and fleeing refugees concluded with a scene of "panic" in Portsmouth Square, "bordered now by Chinatown, by the Italian district, and by the 'Barbary Coast,' a lower tenderloin district." The story noted, "The [Chinese] denizens came out of their underground burrows like rats and tumbled into the square, beating such gongs and playing such noise instruments as they had snatched up. They were met on the other side by the refugees of the Italian quarter. The panic became a madness. At least two Chinamen were taken to the morgue dead of knife wounds, given for no other reason, it seems, than the madness of panic. There are 10,000 Chinese in the quarter and there are thousands of Italians, Spaniards and Mexicans on the other side. It seemed as though every one of these, with the riffraff of the 'Barbary Coast,' made for that one block of open land. The two uncontrolled streams met in the center of the square and piled up on the edges. There they fought all morning, until Regulars restored order with their bayonets."

Claiming "the largest Republican circulation by many thousands of copies a day," the *New York Press* headlined:

HEART OF SAN FRANCISCO IN RUINS;
EARTHQUAKE AND FIRE KILL HUNDREDS;
PROPERTY LOSS $100,000,000 AND GROWING.

Although the *Trenton Times* of New Jersey gave three-fourths of its front page to local stories about a theft of a wagonload of pottery from the Thomas Maddocks' Sons Company [an inside job], burglaries of three homes in the town of Crosswicks, and a squabble between two leaders of the Daughters of the American Revolution, the West Coast disaster received a double-column and a banner headline:

TERRIBLE EARTHQUAKE IN SAN FRANCISCO
THREATENS DESTRUCTION OF CITY

Publishing an "Extra," the *Berkeley Reporter* blared "City A Roaring Furnace," but also erroneously headlined "Los Angeles Razed By A Great Earthquake."

In London, England, the *Guardian* exclaimed:

EARTHQUAKE IN SAN FRANCISCO
Many hundreds in lives lost * The city in flames *
Wholesale destruction of buildings

Incorrectly reporting that the quake lasted three minutes, the story continued:

> In that brief space of time thousands of buildings were either damaged or destroyed, and several hundred persons killed. The city was virtually cut off from communication with the rest of the continent, owing to the collapse of all the telegraph wires except one; all the lighting arrangements were thrown out of gear, and save for the fires which broke out in numberless streets the whole place was in darkness.
>
> The fires spread rapidly, owing to the impossibility of getting water from the burst mains, and in order to limit the area of destruction it was found necessary to blow up several buildings. The telegraph operators were compelled to abandon the Post-Office, because it was partially wrecked, and the operating-room was rendered useless. The first hint of the disaster was contained in a Reuter's telegram from Chicago announcing that the telegraph companies were entirely without communication with San Francisco, and that the Sacramento office of the Western Telegraph Company reported a heavy earthquake in the West. A little later the Kansas City postal authorities received from Los Angeles a report that 1,000 lives had been lost at San Francisco, and another dispatch stated that the city had been practically wrecked. Brief telegrams from Chicago, New York, and other towns followed later in rapid succession, and left no room for doubt as to the awful effects of the visitation.

The *Chicago American* carried the previously noted account by Helen Dare, including her encounter with a member of the Conreid Opera Company. He described the fire destroying the Grand Opera House and quipped, "Sudden close to the opera season, isn't it?"

Subscribers to newspapers receiving dispatches from the Associated Press news service read stories filed by J. M. "Jerry" Carroll. He and his wife were awakened in their house at Eleventh and

Market Street opposite the Majestic Theater by bricks and mortar raining onto their bed. Carroll took his wife to the home of a friend a mile away, then headed for the downtown office of Associated Press Superintendent Paul Cowles. By Wednesday night, the AP office, Jerry recalled, was "on a doorstep in Chinatown, and the copy was written in the glare of conflagration–a light that cost $1,000 per second."

Determined to "get the story," Jerry found himself trudging wherever the news took him, through streets of red-hot cobblestone and bricks, fallen buildings, twisted metal, dust, smoke and cinders, to the waterfront telegraph connection to Oakland. Told by an operator to keep his story to five hundred words, he felt that he could "just as well condense the Bible into a half a column as I could have confined the news of that day into the space." With a bit of Irish beguiling, he persuaded the telegrapher to allow "a few hundred words more."

Since being rousted from bed in his hotel and helping in efforts to rescue his neighbors, James Hopper of the *Call* had been all over the city in his pursuit of who, what, where, when, why, and how. This was the greatest news story of his career, one that he believed could never be equaled. And it certainly was not likely to be surpassed in terms of devastation of property, loss of life, injuries, and human interest stories. On his way downtown, he recalled, "the sun was rising behind a smoky pall already floating above the populous district south of Market Street. The *Call* building was unmarred by the earthquake, and so was the building of the *Examiner* across Third Street from the *Call*, and that of the *Chronicle*, across Market Street from the *Examiner*." Greeted excitedly by acting-City Editor Fred R. Bowie, Hopper was told, "The Brunswick Hotel at Sixth and Folsom is down with hundreds inside her. You cover that."

With the floor of the editorial room ankle-deep in water from ruptured pipes, Hopper grabbed a handful of paper and a few pencils and started up Third Street. Burning buildings tumbled all around him, burying occupants and leaving them helpless and hopeless to face death by the encroaching fire. "The flames swept over them," Hopper would write, "while the saved looked on impotently." He recognized that the story of San Francisco on Wednesday, April 18, 1906, was far more than the fate of the Brunswick Hotel, or even beyond the crucible of South of Market. Hopper flagged down an automobile driven by a youth who embodied the verve, wealth, and ostentatious self-indulgence of an era that Mark Twain had disdainfully called "the Gilded Age." He offered the youth fifty dollars to become his "chauffeur" for the entire day, and the young man "jumped," providing, Hopper wrote, "another example of the twisted vision of us all [on that morning], which refused to acknowledge the true stupendousness of what was happening."

With hired wheels to take him wherever he wished to go, Hopper chose to check on his friends in the Latin Quarter, a picturesque district of narrow streets with low brick buildings built in pioneer days. He found the buildings wrecked with exposed interiors as if they were dollhouses or a stage setting. Among them was the home of friend and fellow writer, Henry Laffler.

"Beneath the pyramid of bricks that had been the front of the building," Hopper wrote, "a dead Chinaman lay, one long yellow hand stretched out of the loose sleeve of his blouse. But a note pinned upon the remnants of the stairs told me that Laffler was safe. I went to the studio of [Xavier] Martinez, the painter. The old building still stood. The studio was full of bricks, but a neatly stacked pile of paintings in the center told me that the painter was safe. How these men escaped is beyond my imagination."

After "whizzing" back to the *Call*, Hopper was told by Bowie to team with another reporter, "Scotty" Morrison, and a cub reporter to cover the progress of the fire and get a list of the dead. Upon leaving the *Call* building, Hopper saw the Grand Opera House, where a few hours before he had listened to Caruso, "burning with explosive violence." As he and his companions roamed the downtown district and found it full of refugees, he was amazed by their immobility and stoicism.

"On each side, like the claws of a crab," he wrote, "the fire was closing in upon them." Yet they sat motionless, "as if cast of bronze, as if indeed they were wrought upon some frieze representing the Misery of Humanity."

In a moment of shock and horror, Hopper gazed at the *Call* building, the tallest in the city, "glowing like a phosphorescent worm" while "cataracts of pulverized fire poured out of a thousand windows." The nearby *Examiner* building was also burning.

While James Hopper and reporters for the city's other papers—the *Bulletin*, the *Chronicle*, and the *Examiner*—were on the streets covering all aspects of the disaster, the quake and subsequent fires, William Randolph Hearst paced the office of his New York newspaper, the *American*. Still fuming over the perceived military censorship of his *Examiner* reporters, he was also frustrated because his New York paper had no photograph of the blazing city by the bay. He wanted a photo to enhance the sensational writing on the front page that his editors were busily composing to attract readers to the *American*.

Ever a resourceful figure, and rarely a man to quibble over journalistic ethics, Hearst saw no difference between a great fire in one city and a conflagration in the city he called his hometown. So why couldn't the talented men in the art department of the *American* dig out a photo of the Baltimore fire of 1904 and do a bit of touching up that would result in the transformation of that waterfront city into San Francisco? Along with a reputation for innovative journalism, which many in America credited (or blamed) for the United States declaring war on Spain in 1898 in order to "Remember the *Maine*" and grab Cuba and the Philippines for America, W. R. Hearst basked in a carefully cultivated picture of himself as a man who could put a finger on a good cause, and incidentally sell a lot of newspapers.

Putting on that hat, Hearst would organize "relief trains" to rumble toward the stricken city of San Francisco. And when the timing was right, he would appear in the city himself with $200,000, garnered through a public fund-raising campaign.

But as these plans were aborning in Hearst's fertile imagination, he was informed that his first newspaper, the San Francisco *Examiner*, had become a victim of fire. Not since he had taken over the paper, he had proudly boasted, did the *Examiner* not appear on the streets and doorsteps of San Francisco. Certainly, no earthquake, no matter how destructive it was, would be permitted to besmirch that record. Even if the *Examiner* building was on fire, there was no reason on earth why it should not be available as usual on Thursday, April 19, 1906.

Consequently, when the owner of the San Francisco *Chronicle*, Michael de Young, offered the use of the *Chronicle*'s editorial facilities and presses to the *Examiner* and the *Call*, it was accepted. The plan was for the three papers to appear as one in an extra edition. But as the staffs worked feverishly to produce a *Call-Chronicle-Examiner*, listed alphabetically on the unique masthead, the water supply that drove the *Chronicle* presses was cut off. To cope with this new disaster, a delegation from the three papers rushed to Oakland and the offices of its afternoon paper, the *Tribune*. Its owner, W. Dargie, agreed to make his presses available. The result was the appearance on Thursday of a hybrid paper with the headline:

EARTHQUAKE AND FIRE:
SAN FRANCISCO IN RUINS

Although the *Call*, *Chronicle*, and *Examiner* newspapers had pulled off an historic journalistic feat, they had been scooped by a four-year-old newspaper that, compared to these three giants, was no more than a journalistic pygmy. Yet, when power went out at the San Francisco *Daily News*, the paper shifted operations to R. V. Rooney's small printing shop at 1308 Mission Street. Using a hand-cranked press capable of printing only single sheets, the harried staff managed to turn out a one-page "Extra," making the *Daily News* the only San Francisco newspaper published on the day of the earthquake, with the headline: "Hundreds Dead!"

A sub-headline read:

Fire Follows Earthquake, Laying Downtown
Section in Ruins–City Seems Doomed
For Lack of Water

One column listed names and circumstances of deaths and injuries underneath sub-headlines of "Known Dead," "Other Dead," and "Injured." The other two columns described scenes of destruction and damage. As long as copies were available, the paper was free to anyone who wanted it.

San Franciscans who managed to find a copy of the *Call-Chronicle-Examiner* read a story that began, "Death and destruction have been the fate of San Francisco." Although the account provided a comprehensive picture of what had occurred, and continued to unfold, the story stated that at nine o'clock on Wednesday morning, "under special order from President Roosevelt, the city was placed under martial law."

The constitutional Commander in Chief of the Army had issued no such directive.

Ten

❦

WHO'S IN CHARGE HERE?

❦

*P*RESIDENT THEODORE ROOSEVELT WAS very familiar with the name of the brigadier general who had ordered troops from the Presidio into the devastated streets of San Francisco on April 18, 1906. As the leader of the Rough Riders in the Spanish-American War in 1898, Roosevelt had gained glory. Fighting under him during action in Cuba, first as a lieutenant and then as a lieutenant colonel, Funston had fought in 22 battles and had his horse shot from under him 17 times.

Three years later as vice-president, Roosevelt wrote to Funston in the Philippines regarding a daring and heroic deed earning him the Congressional Medal of Honor. By then brigadier general of the Twentieth Regiment of the Kansas National Guard, Funston had led 90 Filipinos disguised as rebels and captured the insurgent leader Emilio Aquinado. It was such a dangerous mission that the U.S. Army commander in the Philippines, General Arthur MacArthur (father of Douglas MacArthur), had told Funston, "I fear that I shall never see you again."

Roosevelt was thrilled by Funston's daring and success. On letter-head of the vice president, but sent from Roosevelt's home in Oyster Bay, New York, he wrote to Funston, "This is no perfunctory or formal letter of congratulation. I take pride in this crowning exploit of a career filled with feats of cool courage, iron endurance and gallant daring, because you have added your name to the honor roll of American worthies."

Three months later, Roosevelt again wrote to Funston. This time, he was alarmed. "I hear you think of leaving the Army," he said. "Let me urgently advise you not to do so at the present. I should not expect you to stay in permanently, but I do hope you will remain a couple years more. I think it would be a mistake to get out now unless some altogether exceptional opportunity offers itself. I think you have it in you to rise to very high civil position. I know that what you prize is the chance to do work worth doing, no matter how arduous; and I feel that from both of these standpoints it would be well for you to stay in the Army at present."

Delighted that Funston remained in the Army, still impressed by Funston's record in the Philippines, and now President of the United States, Roosevelt praised Funston in a speech on May 2, 1903, in Manhattan, Kansas–the state where Funston grew up. To agricultural students, many of whom wore uniforms of military cadets, the president who preferred to be known as colonel of the Rough Riders said, "Kansas is full of men who fought the great war [the Civil War], and when in 1898 the appeal to arms came, Kansas farms and Kansas colleges sent forth ten-fold the number of men that were asked for by Uncle Sam; [and] in the Philippines it was given to Kansas to produce one of those men who made marked reputations in the war, in the person of General Funston."

There is no way of knowing if Roosevelt recalled on April 18, 1906, as reports came in that Funston had taken it upon himself to send troops into San Francisco, that five years earlier in the letter of praise to Funston on capturing the rebel leader he'd said, "You have shown qualities which give us good reason to feel that your are fit to perform striking feats of generalship on a much larger scale; if ever the need should arise."

Theodore Roosevelt believed, as poet Thomas Osbert Mordant had written in 1791, that one "crowded hour of glorious life" was worth "an age without a name." Roosevelt's hour had come when he led soldiers in a charge up San Juan Heights in Cuba. For Frederick Funston, it was not a single hour by which he would be judged, but his actions during days of destruction caused by the shaking of ground under a great city and a storm of fire that threatened to consume every mortal and every man-made thing in its path.

Funston realized "that a great conflagration was inevitable, and that the city police force would not be able to maintain the fire-lines and protect public property over the great area affected." Of his actions, he later wrote, "It was at once determined to order out all available troops not only for the purpose of guarding federal buildings, but to aid the police and fire departments of the city." But from the moment the order was issued, a controversy was stirred that would rage across San Francisco in the form of the question, "Who's in charge here?"

While Funston was in overall charge of the troops, demonstrating no hesitation in commandeering elements of the Navy, he insisted that in the early meeting in the cellar of the Hall of Justice, he had acknowledged the preeminence of civil authorities Mayor Schmitz and Police Chief Dinan, as well as acting-Fire Chief John Dougherty. He also delegated direct control of the military to Colonel Charles Morris of the Artillery Corps.

A perhaps inevitable confrontation over jurisdiction between the Army and city officials took place over how to carry out the dynamiting of buildings along the east side of Van Ness Avenue. As noted earlier, Mayor Schmitz feared a welter of lawsuits and had requested a legal opinion. After a judge averred that the city had an inherent right to destroy property to prevent the spread of the fire, the question became one of tactics.

As this matter was being debated between Funston and Schmitz, Captain Frank Nichols of fire department Truck No. 4 declared that Chief Dougherty was the only man from whom he should take orders. Watching the ensuing debate, Brigadier General John Koster of the National Guard "strongly urged," in his words, "the advisability of presenting the objections to the mayor, to enable him to modify or change orders if such a conclusion should be arrived at."

Ultimately, it was Colonel Morris who broke the deadlock by going ahead with the demolitions on Van Ness Avenue. When the tactic of creating a firebreak ultimately failed, Funston informed the War Department, "Fire crossed Van Ness Avenue to the west. Almost certain now entire city will be destroyed."

Another witness to the dispute between Schmitz and Funston was a reporter for the Associated Press. When his account of the conflict reached Washington, D.C., Secretary of War Taft shot off a telegram to Funston. Dated April 21, long after the houses on Van Ness Avenue had been destroyed either by explosions or fires, it said:

> Word comes to the Associated Press that you and Mayor Schmitz are having some conflict of jurisdiction in respect to police matters. Of course as long as you are assisting him, his orders must control. And you must merely conform to his judgment so far as police matters are concerned.
>
> With respect to army supplies and government property generally, you should listen to and co-operate with him in their distribution. You are responsible for the distribution of supplies and sole judge, ultimately.
>
> Please advise me whether the report of the Associated Press has any foundation. It would be much deplored if you and Schmitz could not get along together. I rely on your good sense to avoid conflict and friction, unless the situation is such that it is impossible for you to harmonize matters and in such case you should advise me before taking final action.

When Funston received this message, he was already fuming over what he considered an outrageous interference from the nation's capital. He was especially infuriated over a telegram from Washington asking him to check into the safety of the sender's friends in San

Francisco. Funston fired back that because of "confusion it has been impossible to locate individuals inquired for but attention will be given to the matter as soon as possible."

On April 22, Mayor Schmitz would reply to Taft's telegram:

> I wish again even in the midst of our great troubles to express my indignation at the presumably malicious and decidedly untruthful suggestion that a conflict exists between General Funston and myself. I wish to emphasize the pleasantness and harmony of our relations and co-operation.

Further troubles for Funston resulted from protests that the soldiers had destroyed huge amounts of liquor in keeping with Colonel Morris's General Order No. 1:

> All liquor, except beer, shall be immediately seized and poured into the gutter of the ground so that it cannot be imbibed. The Commanding Officers shall send details of men under Commissioner Officers for this purpose to where liquor can be found. No property except bottles and casks containing this liquor shall be destroyed.

In carrying out the orders, troops raided 131 places and destroyed an estimated $30,000 worth of liquor. Not until the start of Prohibition under the Eighteenth Amendment to the Constitution in the 1920s would so much booze be spilled in an American city on purpose. One of the raided establishments under Colonel Morris's decree belonged to R. G. Schoder. U.S. Marines, commanded by Lieutenant Sidney W. Brewster, marched into his saloon at the corner of Clay and Fillmore Streets. Reporting that the place was not opened forcibly, and that Schoder let the marines in and was present while the liquor was being destroyed, Brewster denied under oath a charge by the proprietor that instead of dumping the liquor, the Marines sold or gave it away.

In the following weeks, a deluge of such stories from outraged saloon keepers flowed to Washington, D.C., forcing the War Department to open an investigation. The major general who had missed the earthquake because he was at his daughter's wedding in Chicago conducted the probe. As the investigation dragged on for more than a year, Major General A. W. Greely requested that Funston provide an explanation of Colonel Morris's order.

Funston replied (June 13, 1907) that Morris had acted because he "feared disorder," but that Funston was "astonished to learn a few days later" that saloons and groceries in the western portion of the city not in immediate danger "had been broken open and the liquor contained in them destroyed." Although soldiers had done "some of it," Funston contended that most of the work was that of Lieutenant Brewster's U.S. Marines. Funston said, "It was never intended that stores and saloons should be broken open and the liquor in them destroyed and I have never been able to see any possible excuse for the action taken."

Colonel Morris responded that he believed Order No. 1 had been justified. Arguing that "prevailing intemperance would unquestionably have precipitated street fights and riots, involving the certainty of more bloodshed," he explained:

> Rioting and drunkenness by a turbulent element were already rife at places where liquor was procurable, and it was only through prompt and energetic action that such disorders were quelled in their incipiency. As a district commander I was expected and required to preserve order in my district; to do so I was compelled to remove every discovered cause that would logically result in disorder. The police had vanished from the streets. It was a physical impossibility, with the number of soldiers available, to prevent access to liquor by those that would undoubtedly have stolen it. The liquor could not be sold; it could not be given away; it could not be removed to a military reservation or to any place where it would be beyond the reach of the lawless element; its existence was an unfair temptation to

the soldiers, and a distinct menace to good discipline. For these
reasons, it was destroyed.

In 1907, the Judge-Advocate General of the Army disputed
claims by saloon and grocery store owners for compensation. Congress agreed and denied payments.

On October 3, 1906, John Dougherty, noting that he was "Retired First Asst. Chief Engineer, S.F.F.D.," but had been directly in
charge of the department after the injury and ultimate death of Chief
Dennis Sullivan, wrote to President Theodore Roosevelt "a few lines
in commendation of the valuable service and assistance rendered this
community during the conflagration that nearly destroyed our city,
by Brigadier General Frederick Funston."

Dougherty's letter continued:

> General Funston, with whom, in my then official position of
> Acting-Chief Engineer of the San Francisco Fire Department,
> I had the pleasure of coming in contact with during the time
> referred to, proved a man of ever ready resources and prompt
> and effective action, qualifications that were greatly appreci-
> ated during those trying times, and to General Funston and the
> men under his command all credit is due for the splendid ef-
> forts of that occasion, and our government is truly to be con-
> gratulated on the possession of such worthy and competent
> officers in its army.

Having once pleaded with General Funston not to quit the
service, Theodore Roosevelt could not have agreed more.

But on the night of Thursday, April 19, 1906, as Funston gazed
at the flames sweeping down from Nob Hill into the western section
of San Francisco, he feared that Friday's sun would rise over the
ashes of a doomed city.

Eleven

❦

ON THE WATERFRONT

❦

WHEN COMMANDER CHARLES J. BADGER of the U.S. Navy's Sixth Marine District, headquartered at San Francisco, directed his flagship *Chicago*, accompanied by the *Boston* and the *Princeton*, to weigh anchor in San Diego Harbor at 5:45 A.M. on Wednesday, April 18, 1906, their course was to be northwesterly to Long Beach. But four hours and twenty minutes later, the DeForest Wireless Telegraph Station at San Diego signaled press reports of an earthquake in San Francisco to the three ships. With official confirmation of the disaster received from the mayor of San Diego, Badger ordered the *Chicago*'s senior engineer officer, Lieutenant Commander T. W. Kinkaid, to bring the boilers to full steam. The *Boston* and the *Princeton* were signaled to do the same, and to reroute to San Francisco.

Although the coal in the engine rooms of the ships was not of the best quality, and against an adverse current estimated at half-a-knot, the flotilla was soon traveling at over seventeen knots. In constant touch with DeForest wireless stations at San Diego and Los Angeles and government stations at Point Arguello, Farallons, Yerba Buena, and Mare Island, Badger was apprised of the conditions to be expected upon arrival. Badger expressed concerns that the earthquake had changed the geography of the Golden Gate and the bay, and requested that a pilot be standing by at Fort Mason to board the *Chicago* to guide her and the other ships into the harbor.

When they arrived off Fort Mason at six o'clock, Badger sent several officers ashore to find and confer with Army authorities. During that time, a party of sailors was fully equipped and ready to disembark to carry out whatever tasks the Army requested. The Navy would land a battalion at daylight on Friday, April 20. Badger noted in his official report that, as the men waited through the night, the city on the port side of Fort Mason was "in full blaze." He continued:

> The buildings within the limits of the post were in danger. The air was filled with burning cinders which were blown by the wind far into the harbor and all the awnings on board had to be furled and the decks wet down to prevent fire. Thousands of panic stricken, homeless and destitute people thronged the shore in the neighborhood of the Fort. Food was being supplied but there had not yet been time for any well organized system of distribution. Drinking water was difficult to find. All were eager to leave but no transportation was immediately available. The officers quarters at Fort Mason were crowded. Many of those who had been driven from their homes and had acquaintances at the Fort had sought shelter there. Some of them were the families of Navy officers.

Badger told the fort's commanding officer that the *Chicago* would be "glad to offer asylum on board" to those needing it. Eventually, 16 enlisted men and two officers from the *Chicago* would supervise the rescue of 20,000 refugees crowded at the foot of Van Ness Avenue. It would rank as the largest sea evacuation in history until the rescue of stranded British forces in Belgium from Dunkirk early in World War II.

A second Navy landing party of 16, led by Lieutenant L. R. Sargent, joined in the fight with Lieutenant Freeman's sailors to save the Appraisers' Building. Elsewhere, the *Chicago*'s executive officer, Lieutenant Commander William P. White, reported to General Funston. His men were assigned to patrol with orders for "the preservation of order and the protection of life and property." While labors of these sailors could not be witnessed directly by Badger, he left no doubt in his report of his esteem for their efforts. He credited their "gallant and successful" and "intelligent and untiring" work, along with praise for Lieutenant Frederick Freeman and his sailors, "for preventing the spread of the fire along the waterfront."

The outcome of this struggle had been in doubt from the moment of Freeman's arrival on the *Preble* at 10:30 Wednesday morning. While the battle against fires was foremost, he'd had to deal with demands from frantic business owners who were desperate to save valuable property. Among these pleas was a request from officials of the Southern Pacific Railroad that Freeman's men save 150 freight cars on a spur of track from Lombard Street to waterfront freight sheds. Most held produce, but five of them contained live chickens. To a demand that he "liberate" the birds and turn them over to the crowd on the docks, Freeman replied that he had "neither the time nor men to do so at this time."

On hearing that crews of German and British ships were looting other railway cars and filling their holds with booty, Freeman investigated. Finding the report untrue, he talked to officers of the ships and requested that their crews protect the freight cars, "as this was a very valuable food supply for the city." Coming "gallantly to the rescue," Freeman reported, was Captain Anderson of the ship *Mayfield*. He not only "did splendid work in saving property" by lending men to the fire-fighting effort, but used his ship as a refuge for women and the elderly.

Among men with business interests on and around the docks was Abraham Ruef. While his political protege, Mayor Eugene Schmitz, was grappling with a city in ruins and on fire, the man who had envisioned himself a political king-maker and a future United States Senator had rushed to the waterfront to beg Freeman to save Ruef's properties on Montgomery Avenue above Broadway, especially his Commercial Hotel. Informed that the lack of water had resulted in a decision to use dynamite to create firebreaks, Ruef produced a supply of the explosive.

Edward M. Lind, an executive of the Hotaling liquor company, was present at this time. He recalled the scene 20 years later in an article in *Argonaut* magazine. He wrote, "If these efforts had proved successful, our chances in the block lower down the hill would have been greatly improved. But they were not successful. Presently the flames for their grip of the structure [the Commercial Hotel] and it went the way of the rest."

Lind's account continued, "Toward dawn on Friday the wind shifted. Where earlier in the night there had been but little breeze save from the draught caused by the conflagration, a stiff westerly wind now blew up. The fire also shifted. It curled along the foot of Telegraph Hill, and thence headed back, south, in our direction. This was a bad fire. The shacks were like tinder, and a whole block would be destroyed in thirty minutes."

Racing to envelop the Barbary Coast, the flames had eaten through a block on Pacific Street and buildings to the north. According to an article in the *Call* on May 12, 1906, a group of "dissolute males" and women "painted and dressed in their gaudiest finery" had abandoned the saloons and brothels and congregated on the steps of the U.S. Mint to throw a party. When a wagon carrying crates of champagne and other fine liquors rattled by, it was attacked and looted, resulting in a "wilder, fiercer orgie [*sic*] than the red light district had ever known."

Noting that the menace to the waterfront was at its worst at the corner of Jackson Street and Montgomery, Lind described the threat to the Eiffel Tower Restaurant building on the northeast corner. Higher than any structure in the area, it was in "full blaze, and the sparks from this fire threatened at any moment to start another blaze in an old lodging house across the street on the southeast corner, which was part of our [Hotaling Company] block."

When the Eiffel Tower building collapsed, Lind was relieved that his firm's building was unscathed, and the "danger from that source was ended." But nearly all the low buildings on the north side of Jackson Street, from Montgomery to Battery Street, were wiped out.

It was three o'clock in the afternoon when Lieutenant Freeman noted the wind shift. It "commenced to blow a gale from the northwest and swept the fire around the North Beach end of the waterfront and the southern end of Telegraph Hill with great velocity." An hour earlier, the fire fighting seemed to have "progressed favorably." Now it came at the Filbert Street dock from the neighborhood of the Appraisers' Building, along Vallejo Street, and from the north in the direction of Meigg's Wharf, consuming sheds along the way. To try to stop it from coming down to the waterfront, Freeman "deemed it advisable" to go to Pier 27 and employ the boats *Leslie* and *Active* to attempt to save grain sheds at North Point. At this time, he recalled, "it seemed that the whole waterfront was doomed."

Freeman and his men found they had more on their hands than a gigantic fire; they had the task of "policing the territory" in which they worked. Freeman reported "great trouble" on East Street (now the Embarcadero) controlling people "hysterically endeavoring to escape the flames." They surged down East Street "at frantic speed over hose lines, bursting the over-worked hose at frequent intervals." Freeman found it necessary to station sentries at all corners with orders to "shoot down horses whose owners drove over a hose faster than a walk."

When fresh men were needed, the *Active* was sent to the *Chicago* with a request for relief crews. The sailors joined in a battle that Freeman called "the hardest fight we had during the fire at this point." A sulfur works was burning. The gale wind sent showers of cinders, some of them three- and four-inches square, and making the spot "a purgatory."

Freeman strategically used his fire boats to pump water from the harbor and create a spray that would act as a blanket to both smother the cinders and soak shed rooftops and pier planking. When hot cinders fell on the decks of the boats, the crews had to turn their hoses on themselves. The need for fire fighters was so desperate that the *U.S.S. Perry's* Chinese cook was ordered out of his galley and on deck to help man a hose.

One of Freeman's men who watched him pacing the docks and shouting encouragement recalled, "He looked all in, with the sweat streaking down through the grime on his weather-beaten face onto the dirty white handkerchief he had tied around his neck." In lauding Freeman as "a born leader of men, a skipper whose men would go to hell and back for him," the officer's account was one voice in a large chorus of praise for Freeman's leadership and courageousness that formed a consensus that, without him, the waterfront would have been a total loss. Yet, in his report to the Commander-in-Chief, Pacific Squadron, Freeman listed 24 individuals by name–civilian, military, naval, and city employees–and crews of boats and ships in general, along with members of the fire department, as deserving the credit.

Twelve

GLORIOUS BATTLE

*O*HEN CITY APPRAISER JOHN T. DARE reached the Appraisers' Building at Sansome and Jackson Streets at eight o'clock on the morning of the quake, he found the aging, squat, and not very pretty structure intact. But fire was moving toward its Washington Street end.

In this moment of impending peril, Dare was grateful that the building's planners had installed a 5,000-gallon tank on the roof that drew water from the property's artesian well. When employees known as attachés arrived, he ordered them to stand by with filled buckets. Others armed with mops and wet sacks were stationed at all windows to douse drifting embers that might fall onto the wooden sills. Joining in the effort were Customs House employees and workers from Station B of the U.S. Post Office on Jackson Street.

"This work was kept up throughout the day," the *Chronicle* noted, "and by nightfall the fighters, completely fatigued by a hard day's toil, were rewarded with an assurance of success by the flames dying down on the low and dynamited Washington Street buildings. All night a patrol watched the roof of the building and guarded the water tank with the same care and caution as though it were a bank vault."

Sentries with buckets, mops, and axes patrolled the surrounding blocks of stores and warehouses. Others were posted on the rooftops of adjacent structures to smother wind-blown cinders and to chop away any burning cornices.

On Thursday, the building was never in danger, but the shifting of the wind on Friday would put it in its most serious jeopardy since John Dare arrived on Wednesday morning. Rallying with their buckets and mops, the wearied guardians resumed posts at windows and on the roof. But now allies from the Army, Navy, and fire department joined them in a pitched struggle to beat back a fire freshly aroused and energized by gale winds.

With the Appraisers' Building and Station B of the Post Office saved, John Dare told a *Chronicle* reporter, "The precision and determination with which these firefighters worked is beyond description. Never, even in war, did the soldiers and marines face the dangers they encountered in their glorious battle with flames, and never did the patriotic spirit of a few citizens and government employees rise to such a height as when those soot and smoke-grimed warriors, all but exhausted, came back to their superior officers and with the proper salute informed them that the danger had passed and the section [of the city] was saved. If no official recognition is given to these men, their uphill victory will go down in the history of the city as one of the most remarkable and self-sacrificing acts of the calamity."

The same could be said about the San Franciscans who saved the U.S. Mint. Among them was its superintendent. A former newspaperman and the beneficiary of a political patronage system that decided who got what government job, Frank Aleomon Leach had rushed from his home in Oakland to become one of the first to walk through the inferno of the South of Market area early on Wednesday morning. He hurried amid the tumult and chaos of Market Street toward the Mint, located at Fifth and Mission Streets.

Built in 1874, it was to be a stolid symbol of the might and majesty of a post-Civil War United States that spanned a continent and believed there were no bounds on the bright future of American enterprise, democracy, and a capitalist system, to which San Francisco was a Golden Gate on the Pacific Coast.

Eleven years after the harrowing events of April 18, 1906, Leach would draw on his writing talent to produce an autobiography. In a chapter of *Recollections of a Newspaperman*, he gave a detailed, vivid, and self-conscious account of "the most exciting feature of my administration of the mint in San Francisco."

After describing his hazardous trek through the crumbled and burning city to reach the Mint, he wrote:

> I found that I had also reached the end of the fire zone. A lot of small buildings directly opposite the mint building on Fifth Street had already been destroyed by the flames, and the fire was slowly eating its way northerly toward the Metropolitan Temple and Lincoln school building, both of which faced Fifth Street; besides, from the center of the same block it was working its way more rapidly toward the big Emporium Building. Another branch of flames had swept the buildings on the south side of Mission opposite the mint building, and was crossing Mission, heading for Market Street, clearly pointing out for destruction all the big buildings west and north of the mint; and it was also evident that before the afternoon was over the two fires would come together on Fifth Street, and thus cut off the mint building from communication with the outside world and surround it with fire, if not destroy it.

When Leach entered the Mint, he was "greatly pleased" to find fifty employees "whose sense of loyalty to duty had not been modified by fear of the earthquake or the horror of being penned up in a big building surrounded by fire." He also found that night watch captain, T. W. Hawes, and others had fought to keep the fire from getting a foothold in the Mint Building from the east and west sides.

Surveying the situation from the roof at one in the afternoon and finding it "perilous," Leach thought it improbable that the Mint could "withstand that terrific mass of flames that was sweeping down upon us from Market Street." As he'd feared, two lines of fire had merged. "It had thus marshaled the elements of destruction and was now marching them down on the mint building," he recalled. "The battle would soon be on."

The battle would not be fought by the Mint employees alone. Lieutenant A. G. Armstrong of the U.S. Army, Leach wrote in a condescending manner, "was thoughtful enough to bring a squad of ten soldiers from Fort Miley to help in any way the men could be of service to us." The soldiers joined the fifty Mint workers, divided into a squad for each floor. Because of a newly-installed system of pipes and a pump that drew water from an artesian well to a pair of tanks on the roof, and had been installed with fire hydrants, the teams had plenty of water. The greatest threat to the men in the building, Leach felt, would be the intense heat from outside. Accordingly, he devised a plan of retreat but decided not to tell it to the men until such time as it might be needed.

Leach's account of the threat to the Mint continued:

> We had scarcely finished placing the men, when, inside, the building was made almost dark as night by a mass of black smoke that swept in upon us just ahead of the advancing flames; then, following, came a thunderous shower of red hot cinders, big and small, which fell on our building as thick as hail in a storm, and piled up on the roof in drifts nearly two feet deep at one place. The court in the center of the building was open to the sky, and in it were much wood and timber. Here the sparks and cinders fell as thick as elsewhere. A dozen little fires were starting in the court, and the men with the hose streams at each end of the court had all they could do to keep those fires down and new ones from starting.

Assisting in meeting this threat, Leach found his clothing and hat singed, but his growing fear was that the Mint "was doomed to destruction." When the "shower of living coals" abated, he left the courtyard and went to the top floor. He found buildings across an alley ablaze. Flames shot against the Mint Building as if by "a huge blow-pipe." Window glass "melted like butter."

"The heat was now intense," Leach wrote. "It did not seem possible for the structure to withstand this terrific onslaught. The roar of the conflagration and crashing and falling buildings together with the noise given off from the exploding [flaking of sandstone walls] of our building were enough to strike terror in our hearts, if we had had time to think about it."

The account continued:

At times the concussions from the explosions were heavy enough to make the floor quiver. Once I thought a portion of the northern wall and roof had fallen in, so loud and heavy was the crashing noise. Great tongues of flame flashed into open windows where the glass had been melted out, and threatened to seize upon the woodwork of the interior of the tier of rooms around that side of the building. Now came the climax. Would we succeed in keeping the fire out, or should we have to retreat and leave the fire fiend to finish the destruction of the mint unhindered? Every man was alive to the situation, and with hose and buckets of water they managed to be on hand at every place when most needed—first in this room and then in that.

The men in relays dashed into the rooms to play water on the flames; they met a fierce heat; though scorched was their flesh, each relay would remain in these places, which were veritable furnaces, as long as they could hold their breaths, then come out to be relieved by another crew of willing fighters. How long this particular feature of the contest went on I have little idea, but just when we thought we were getting the best of the fight another cloud of dense, black, choking smoke suddenly joined the flames and drove us back to the other end of the building, and some of the men, more sensitive to the stifling smoke, were compelled to go to the floors below.

I thought the building was now doomed, beyond question, but to our surprise the smoke soon cleared up and the men, with a cheer, went dashing into the fight again. Every advantage gained by them was told by their yells of exultation. We were gaining in the fight when word came to me that the roof was now on fire and the flames were getting beyond the control of the men there, who only had buckets to fight with. The roof men wanted a hose stream, but I sent word back that the hose was needed on the third floor for a while longer and that as soon as we were out of danger at this point we would attack the roof fire from underneath in the attic. I knew the roof would burn slowly, as it was covered with copper roofing plates.

The explosions of the stones in our walls grew fainter, and finally we heard no more of them. The flames ceased their efforts to find entrance to our stronghold through the windows, but the heat reflected from the mass of red hot ruins to the north of us was almost unbearable: we could not see what the situation was outside, or tell just what other or further experience was in store for us. However, we began to feel that the fight was nearly won and that, after all, we were going to save the building. We were now able to keep the interiors of the rooms which were most threatened wet down by the bucket men, so I sent the men with the hose to extinguish the roof fire, which was quickly done. In a half hour or so our defensive work was over. I now bad [*sic*] time to take some observations, and made a trip over the building for that purpose. I found that the building had not been seriously injured, and that with careful watching and preventing the lodgment of cinders, there would be no further danger of the mint being destroyed. The fight was won. The mint was saved.

We were a happy band, pleased with the result of our efforts in successfully fighting off the fire, but we did not think so much of our victory, until a day or two later when we saw the benefits to follow to the stricken community in a financial way.

We opened the only available vaults in the city holding any considerable amount of coin.

It was now near 5 o'clock in the evening [Wednesday]. The struggle with the fire demon had lasted from early morning, and all were tired, but there were other duties to be performed by them, as no relief crew was obtainable. The men were divided in watches, which gave some of them opportunity to obtain a little rest. The watch on duty was stationed at the exposed places. The hose lines were stretched, filled buckets were placed in convenient places, and steam pressure in the boiler room was ordered kept up so the pumps could be started at a moment's notice if needed.

When all the preparations and plans for the night had been arranged I determined to make the effort to go to Oakland and send a report to the Director of the mint at Washington, as I knew the authorities there would be pleased to know that our building had been saved. I shall never forget the feeling that came over me as I descended the steps of the mint building into Fifth Street and noted the change that had taken place there within a few short hours. When I passed down that block on Fifth Street from Market in the morning all the large business blocks, from the Metropolitan Temple and the Lincoln school were intact. The soldiers, policemen, firemen, and privileged citizens moving to and fro then gave animation to the scene, but now, turn which way you would, the view presented was one of utter ruin, desolation, and loneliness. The buildings just described were piles of smoking and blazing ruins. The street was encumbered with fallen trolley poles and tangled wires and other indestructible debris from the burned buildings. Not a human being was to be seen. It seemed as if all the people and buildings of the city but the mint and its defenders had been destroyed. It was a most depressing scene of desolation.

The heat was intense, but I picked my way through the obstacles lying in twisted and tangled masses in the street until I got out of the fire zone. I then started for the ferry at the foot of Market Street, taking something of the course on my return as that by which I came in the morning, although I had to make a wider detour to the north, as the flames had worked several blocks farther in that direction. On my way I saw that part of the fire had escaped from the firemen [on] Sansome street, and was racing across Kearny Street to Dupont, threatening, in its course, the destruction of Chinatown. The poor, unfortunate inmates of this section, realizing the fate in store for their homes and property, were in a state of great activity and excitement.

From the speed the fire was making in their direction and the reluctance some of the Chinamen were showing in the way of leaving their homes and property, I felt that there would be a loss of life here to be added to the list of deaths caused by the disaster, but the soldiers and police came along and drove the loiterers out of the zone of danger. It was an appalling scene that I passed through on my way to the ferry. The wild march of the flames up the hill, the fleeing residents, the rushing of the firemen with their engines and trucks, and of other fire fighters to a new line of defense, the exploding charges of dynamite used to blow down buildings in the path of flames, combined in telling, in a manner stronger than words, the terrible character of the disaster the people of San Francisco were facing.

Arriving in Oakland, Leach went to the telegraph office and sent off a message to the Director of the Mint at Washington, D.C.:

San Francisco visited early this morning by terrible earthquake followed by fire which has burned the greater part of business district. Mint building not damaged much by shock. Every building around the mint burned to the ground. It is the only building not destroyed for blocks. I reached building before the worst of the fire came, finding a lot of our men there, stationed them at points of vantage from roof to basement, and with our fire apparatus and without help from the fire department we successfully fought the fire away, although all the windows on Mint Avenue and back side third story were burned out; fire coming in drove us back for a time. Adjusting rooms and refinery damaged some and heavy stone cornice on that side of building flaked off. The roof burned some little. Lieutenant G. R. Armstrong Sixth United States Infantry with squad of men, was sent to us by commanding officer of department, who rendered efficient aid. Fire still burning in central and western parts of city, and what little remains of central business section is threatened. I could not report sooner, as I had to wait until I could return to Oakland. No dispatches could be sent from San Francisco.

Leach observed "great activity in Oakland among the people in preparing to take care of the thousands of refugees who had so suddenly and unexpectedly been thrown upon the generosity of the community." He wrote, "The churches and all public assembly places were thrown open to the homeless and hungry. Food, bedding, and clothing were provided as if by magic. Thousands of private homes were opened to the sufferers, and no one had occasion to complain. An intelligent organization of Oakland's leading and active citizens was effected in the shortest possible time. Lawyers, merchants, capitalists, preachers, teachers—in truth, people, men and women from all walks of life—were represented in the list of those who responded at once to aid in receiving and caring for the sufferers. Committees were sent to the depot and ferries to receive and direct the sufferers to places of refuge as fast as they arrived within the limits of Oakland. It was a grand and noble work, and was discharged with willingness and enthusiasm. It would take too much space to relate the details of the later organization and work of the citizens in caring for the refugees, the establishment of camps, and the orderly provision for the multitude of people of almost all nationalities. All I can say here is that it was well done, and a credit to the community and humanity of the people composing it."

Returning to San Francisco early Thursday morning, Leach was advised by a policeman at the Ferry Building that fire extended both north and south. Determined to get to the Mint, he found the heat not as great as he expected, but now and then "suffocating clouds of smoke" were so thick he could hardly see or breathe. "Tons and tons of debris" filled the street. But when he turned onto Fifth Street, his heart "thrilled with emotion." Seeing the Stars and Stripes floating from an improvised flagstaff on a gable of the Mint, he believed that the flag "confirmed our victory over the fire demon in the contest of the day before."

The night before in New York City, Mark Twain had taken to the stage of Carnegie Hall on behalf of the Robert Fulton Memorial Association's campaign to raise funds for a monument to the memory of the man who first used a steam engine to power a boat. Twain's speech itself turned out to be historic. He announced that it was to be his last public lecture. "I see many faces in this audience well known to me," he said. "They are all my friends, and I feel that those I don't know are my friends, too. I wish to consider that you represent the nation, and that in saying goodbye to you I am saying goodbye to the nation."

Telling the audience that he wished to deliver "a historical address," he pretended to have forgotten the subject of his speech, then declared that Fulton had invented the dirigible balloon. But at the end, he abandoned the humor that had made him rich, famous, and beloved, to talk of a city he had not visited since 1868. He said, "In the great name of humanity, let me say this final word: I offer an appeal in behalf of the vast, pathetic multitude of fathers, mothers and helpless little children. They were sheltered and happy two days ago. Now they are wandering, forlorn, hopeless, and homeless, the victims of a great disaster. So I beg of you, I beg of you to open your hearts and open your purses and remember San Francisco, the smitten city."

Thirteen

❀

NO PLACE TO GO

❀

O N THE SIDEWALK AROUND THE MINT BUILDING on Friday, April 20, 1906, John Leach found several hundred improvised shelters. The people in these shelters found that the fountains in front of the building were some of the very few supplies of water in the burned-out district. No one could say just how long these makeshift dwellings would serve as their home address.

At the same time, two blocks away in the Beaux Arts U.S. Post Office Building at Seventh and Mission Streets, postal employees were determined to prove that not even an earthquake would stay the city's intrepid mail couriers from making their rounds. As fire had threatened the building, ten workers on the third floor of the building refused the Army's order to evacuate. With the blaze flaring around the building and flames licking its windows and walls, they'd fought back with water-soaked mailbags from the freight elevator's hydraulic lifting system. With the fire danger passed, those ten workers and other postal employees had worked for two days to restore operations.

In consequence of their efforts, a meeting was held on Friday morning with officials of the Post Office, the Postal Inspection Division, and the Railway Mail Service to discuss the restoration of all mail services. Recalling the conference in a series of articles for *Argonaut* magazine, William F. Burke, secretary to the postmaster at the time and later assistant postmaster, noted the unanimous decision that since telegraph service was either out of commission or severely limited, "the first need of stricken citizens of the city was to get word to their friends on the outside that, while they were still alive, they were in great need." Therefore, the Post Office's priority was to collect and expedite outgoing letters. The first step of this process was to commandeer as many wagons and automobiles as possible and dispatch them to collect all mail that had been brought to postal stations across the city.

"These collections during the day were hurried to the main post office," wrote Burke, "where the clerks, after setting their cases upright and re-arranging the disorganized furniture, undertook the distribution of the mail. In the meantime, other wagons were impressed at the Ferry Station, where the mail was piling high, and these [wagons] hauled the incoming sacks to the main office, where it was distributed in readiness for dispatch to the stations."

Automobiles were also sent to pick up letters at refugee camps in Golden Gate Park, at the Presidio, and other parks and open spaces. Signs announcing this service were attached to the fronts of the vehicles. Arriving at a camp in one of the cars, Burke found the effect "electrical." As the people saw the machine, he recalled, "they cheered and shouted in a state bordering on hysteria." At the Presidio, a riot almost occurred as people "crowded around the machine and blocked its progress." To the refugees it was "the first sign of rehabilitation and, as it proceeded, the mail automobile left hope in its wake."

Burke's reminiscence continued:

> The news spread rapidly, and also the fact that the Post Office would handle everything, stamped or unstamped, as long as it had an address to which it could be sent. When I went back in the afternoon, [after] the rounds of the morning to collect mail from the camps, the wonderful mass of communications that

poured into the automobile was a study in the sudden misery that had over-taken the city. Bits of cardboard, cuffs, pieces of wrapping paper, bits of newspapers with an address in the margin, pages of books and sticks of wood all served as a means to let somebody in the outside world know that friends were alive and in need among the ruins.

Altogether we gathered a wagon load of as curious mail as was ever handled; and as it was brought to the machine we threw it into the mail pouches. When we had covered the last camps in the Presidio, the Richmond District and the park, we made our way to the main post office where this curious mail could be distributed in the best possible way to get it to its destination. It came to our knowledge later that not one piece of this mail that was properly addressed failed of delivery.

To deal with this flood of mail, the postmaster required every clerk to work 12-hour days and carriers to work on Sundays, in violation of the law. On Friday, April 20, stamps were on sale at all stations, but if letters came to the main post office without stamps they were still sent out. "No man without money and who trusted the postal service of San Francisco and dropped his un-stamped letter in the mails found he had trusted in vain," Burke noted proudly.

Marshall Stoddard had only his detachable shirt collar on which to write a note to his mother. "This is the closest I can come to paper," he wrote. "Lost all my things, some burnt up and money stolen. Living out of charity at the Presidio."

A letter from Dr. Charles V. Cross to his brother was sent from the First Free Emergency Dispensary on Devisadero Street. Uncertain if a previous note had gotten through, he wrote:

> Just while I have a minute, instead of eating breakfast I will try and send you a few lines to tell you we still live. Ere this I suppose you received my first letter, that was written while the fire still raged. After writing that letter we were in danger again of

being burned out and the real danger did not pass until last night, when a rain came up, and we are now practically safe. As I said, the fire would stop when it consumed all, and so it did. The little district we are now in is all that remains of this city, and most of it is uninhabitable. Many houses are shaken down or are too dangerous to go into.

After relating some of his experiences during the quake and that "damage to the house was not apparently serious, so far as a place for habitation, and after we had righted some of the wreck and eliminated the danger of fire we joined the multitude in the streets for by this time there were thousands in the middle of the street," he continued:

As no buildings in our immediate vicinity were crushed the people seemed good-natured, but the quakes that continued at intervals sent terror to their souls. Everybody joked and laughed and altogether up to that time it looked well, but the picture was soon to change.

On a bike I went down to my office and the picture of desolation increased with every block. Fires on the way had started and desolation was on the way.

The Columbian Building, on the fifth floor of which my office is located, did not have a piece of plaster on it the size of my hand. The front wall was leaning toward the street two feet and the steps in places were loose. The elevators were helpless. I waded though the plaster and debris and found my office like all the rest.

After loading up with what I considered the most valuable articles I started out. On the way down a piece of marble struck me in the back, and with my bundles and typewriter I rolled down about twenty steps, and the typewriter suffered the least of all. For a while I could not move, but the raging fire which was in the block across the street from me soon brought me to my feet.

I staggered to the rear door, which was the only one that could be opened, and stood contemplating what to do when a strong, husky lad walked by with the multitude that was filing past. I grabbed him and asked if he wanted to work. He said "Yes," and with him we moved up a half mile and returned for another load. The fire at this time was across the [Market] street and the beautiful Emporium, Academy of Sciences and Flood Buildings were in flames. Martial law was declared and people were driven back. My Government appointment enabled me to get past with my boy and we got another load. I could not carry a thing, but he was a regular packhorse. We got this load safe, and as the fire had escaped us, and as the other buildings on the other side were gone, we took hope.

I started home and met one of my patients with an auto. With him I returned and got my diploma, some Government books and packages we could not get out on my first trip, and these we took to Miss Danks' house at 2007 Devisadero Street ... I slept like a good dog and the only one in the block that did sleep. I can't write more today. I have treated fully a hundred people while writing this letter and the number is increasing, as it is now raining.

Evidently having money to buy a postage stamp, Ernest H. Adams, a sales representative of jewelry-makers Reed & Barton of Taunton, Massachusetts, wrote to his employers:

At last I am able to pass mail through the lines since the 18th, the morning of the most terrible disaster that ever befell a state or city.

For me to describe the scenes and events of the past few days would be an impossibility at present, and no doubt you would have had more news regarding the awful fate of this city than I myself know. All that I can say at this writing is, that about 5:15 A.M., Wednesday morning, I was thrown out of bed and in a twinkling of an eye the side of our house [at 151–24th Ave.]

was dashed to the ground. How we got into the street I will never be able to tell, as I fell and crawled down the stairs amid flying glass and timber and plaster. When the dust cleared away I saw nothing but a ruin of a house and home that it had taken twenty years to build. I saw the fires from the city arising in great clouds and it was no time to mourn my loss so getting into what clothing I could find, I started on a run for [115] Kearny St., five miles away.

Reaching the office, I waded through plaster, etc., to find the goods still in the cases but off the shelves without any damage being done them. Locking the doors again I rushed to [the] street to find the city two blocks away in flames and the fire department helpless, as all of the water mains had been ruptured and destroyed. I gathered up a force of seven men, stationed them at our office doors, and started for a truck, after hunting an hour I secured a truck at $50.00 a load and again started for the office. Fortunately I had two guns in the office, and stationing one man at the entrance and one on the truck with orders to shoot, the balance of us went to work, and that dray man pulled the heaviest load of his life. I saved all of the Sterling Hollow and Flat Ware with the exception of a few Flat Ware samples in the trays beside my books, stock sterling and plated ware books. The plated ware, it was impossible to touch, as the flames were then upon us, and another truck at $1,000.00 a load was an impossibility.

By this time the streets were a pandemonium, and locking office doors we mounted our guarded load and started for the country out toward the Cliff House. My house being in ruins I knew not where I would land, but I kept the teamster going with a gun at his back until we were three miles out of town. Meeting a friend, I placed the goods in the parlor of his little cottage that had not been damaged much and I thought was safe. Then I hiked for home to see how the wife was. I found her sitting beside the ruins of what was once her home.

All Wednesday night we guarded the treasure, but the fire kept creeping toward us, driving the people back to the Cliff House, the western extremity of the Peninsula, and Thursday I was again forced to move the goods westward. The last stand was our back yard, two miles from the first stand, and I am now with our sterling goods, the remains of our beautiful office.

The city is under martial law and we are living on the government, or at least many are. As soon as the goods were safe, I cleaned out the nearest grocery store of canned goods and we are living in a tents [*sic*], cooking means on a few bricks piled up Dutch-oven style. Will endeavor to get into [the] city tomorrow, but every man caught in town is placed at work clearing the streets and they are kept at work until they drop.

With this valuable property under my care I could not afford to take any chances, and I have stayed close to my cache.

I have had plenty to do, as hundreds are without shelter and little clothing.

One of our prominent attorneys is camped near us and he has advised me that I did the right thing in saving what I could for you, and he said that it will not affect our insurance any and it is only necessary to make affidavit to what stock we had at the time of the fire, and the possibility is that nearly all the insurance companies are broke by this time.

The city is a mass of ruins from the Ferry Building or water front to Van Ness Ave., and across town from north to south. Within the above radius not business house [*sic*] is left standing. Dohrmann Commercial Co., Shreve & Co., every jeweler are a thing of the past. Not a hotel in town, restaurant or cafe.

As all of our photo books were destroyed, I would request that you forward me a line as soon as possible....

Will start in and make out a list of what I saved in Sterling and forward it immediately, so that you may present your claim under our insurance policies that you have at the factory.

Adams said in a postscript: "Here we are all paupers together, but we have our grit left."

This attitude was abundantly noted by *Bulletin* reporter Pauline Jacobson, as she toured refugee camps. In an article entitled "How it Feels to be a Refugee and Have Nothing in the World" she wrote, "It is truly remarkable the airs that some of these refugees take unto themselves these days. It is no use trying to get ahead especially of those favored of fortune who escaped in nothing but a dressing gown and slippers. Talk about the earthquake being a common leveler. It is nothing of the sort. It has only turned things upside down. There is as much class distinction as ever, but now-a-days it's your Weary Willie [tramp] who's on top. It is he who is your mushroom aristocracy, while the underdog is the man so poverty stricken as to know no other experience save the luxurious repose in a brass bedstead on a white curled hair mattress." In the "grand exodus of men, women and children," Jacobson discovered "little of excitement." She decided that, in part, it was the pathological calm of a partial emotional paralysis, but in the main was "the healthy calm" of a "new joy" in finding that everybody was a friend. "The individual, the isolated self was dead," she wrote. "And that is the sweetness and gladness of the earthquake and fire" that sprang forth "not of bravery, nor of strength, nor of joy in a new city, but of a new inclusiveness."

Another observer of the melting of social barriers, Adolf Sinsheimer, wrote to a friend in a letter, "White people and Negroes and Chinese and Japanese all mixed without prejudice—one bench in the park might harbor all the chief races and no one seemed to be aware of it. One feeling seemed to possess all of them, and the expression was the same on everyone's face—a dull staring look of resigned despair—a waiting for the end—fear—hopelessness. I never before saw people so cling to one another with a complete surrender of individuality."

There is no doubt that Jacobson and Sinsheimer had discerned the milk of human kindness flowing in the refugee camps and the shattered streets of San Francisco. But it would not be lasting. As the ashes cooled and the work of carting away rubble began, divisions of class and race would reappear and prove as ugly as the cracks and crevices that had suddenly opened in the streets and walls of buildings on the morning of April 18, 1906.

Meanwhile, the shock and trauma of abrupt rootlessness was met in as many ways as there were homeless; from the opportunist thief who'd tried to make off with Caruso's luggage and looters leaping through broken windows of shattered storefronts to carry off everything they could hold; James Hopper helping to extricate strangers from a collapsing building; sailors and firemen struggling to save Hotaling's whiskey; to Madame Fremstad of the Metropolitan Opera Company of New York buying sausages for displaced persons in Union Square. For each act of lawlessness or meanness there were scores of instances of kindness, caring, helping hands, comforting shoulders to cry on, laughter amid tears, and even songs. In a camp established among tombstones and vaults in Woodland Burial Park, a refugee who'd dragged a saved piano from his home teamed with a vaudeville musical act to render ragtime tunes. On a nearby curb an old man played fiddle. Elsewhere, as a growing mass of consuming flames seemingly bent on leaving nothing of San Francisco but memories of gaudy days and bawdy nights, a woman with another rescued piano sang "There'll Be a Hot Time in the Old Town Tonight."

Fourteen

FURY OF THE EARTH DRAGON

N 1848, BEFORE GOLD WAS DISCOVERED at Sutter's Mill, California, no more than twenty Chinese could be found in all of the United States. Because laborers were needed to dig mines and later to lay track for the Central Pacific Railroad, immigrants from China arrived in tens of thousands, with the expectation among their white employers that when their cheap labor was no longer required, they would return to China. But when the gold rush faded and the railroad was completed, the number who remained was magnified by a continuing influx of Chinese enticed by the prospect of earning money in America to support not only themselves, but also their families in their homeland. On April 18, 1906, the Chinese population of San Francisco was estimated at sixty thousand. The area to which they were confined and that the whites had named "Chinatown" (the first in the United States) lay on the eastern slope of Nob Hill. This residential area of the city's early settlers was, noted one historian, "commanding and picturesque."

Nine blocks extending from Kearny Street on the east to Powell Street on the west and from Pacific Street on the north and Clay Street on the south, Chinatown was close to Portsmouth Square and the Hall of Justice. Stretching from Pacific Street across Telegraph Hill to Union Street was the Latin Quarter. Home to many of James Hopper's artistic friends, there were more than thirty thousand French, Italian, and Mexican residents. Eastward from Kearny Street and northward along Pacific Street sprawled the Barbary Coast.

Contemporary historian Charles Eugene Banks wrote that Chinatown was "famed among the travelers of the world as one of the greatest points of interest in San Francisco." The *Baedeker Guide* advised that "no one should leave the city without visiting it" and that strangers could do so "unattended without danger" during the day, "but the most interesting time to visit it is at night when everything is in full swing until after midnight." The travel book recommended that "a regular guide" accompany nocturnal explorers. These guides, generally detectives who could be procured at hotels, charged five dollars for a party of not more than six sightseers.

Travelers to San Francisco tingled with the same excitement felt by tourists to New York when they dared to explore that city's infamous Bowery and a rough area of saloons and dens of vice called the "Tenderloin." The most exotic and strange places in San Francisco's Chinatown were the Joss Houses, "where visitors are expected to buy bundles of scented incense tapers." Of the most famous of these places, the Joss House of the Suey Sings, historian Charles Banks provided this description:

> The fittings of this place were exceedingly rich and elaborate. The joss, or god, hideous of face and form, but splendid in finery, sat on his haunches beneath a canopy of gold cloth of rare design and bearing the device of the sacred dragon in burnished gold thread, while at either hand stood solid hammered silver urns, bowls, and vessels used in mystical Celestial worship. Behind the figure were ranged stands of spears and weapons of every description brought from the temples of China, and all of exquisite workmanship and great antiquity. These stands were flanked by banners of almost solid gold, beautifully garnished

and covered with hieroglyphics worked in silver and gold thread, the whole contributing to make the picture one of oriental splendor seldom seen outside the sacred temples at Pekin.

Life in Chinatown was "of a kaleidoscopic nature," exemplified by "the feast of the dragon" on New Year's Day, when all debts must be eliminated and the slate cleaned for the coming year. The day was celebrated with a long paper dragon and "the beating of tom-toms, the squeaking of reed instruments and the shouting of the fanatical populace" in scenes that were "weird and highly impressive." Even more fascinating, "but repulsive to people of taste and refinement," was Chinatown's "underground." Here, white San Franciscans believed, the Chinese "burrowed like rats, and countless tunnels, foul-smelling and repellent, were thronged with opium-smoking hordes."

This was the Chinatown in which Bret Harte found gambling dens and "ways that are dark and tricks that are vain," in which "the heathen Chinese is peculiar." It was the place in which the white population believed there was traffic of enslaved girls, leading to prolific and endless bloody feuds between Tongs and other mysterious societies.

It was the picture of Chinatown that savvy businessmen eagerly promoted in order to reap money from wide-eyed tourists. Adding to the allure of the exotic and possibly dangerous was the way the Chinese dressed. Clinging to the culture and customs of the land they had left to seek riches in America, they wore traditional outfits of gowns with wide sleeves. With feet in sandals, men wore skullcaps. Their hair dangled in long queues that white people called "pigtails." White people commonly referred to the Chinese people as "chinks."

Among the exotic customs that had puzzled white Christians of San Francisco during previous earthquakes was the Chinese belief that digging holes in the ground and throwing burning sacred papers into them would appease the "Earth Dragon." And so, when the ground shook in the early morning on April 18, the terrified people of Chinatown raced into the streets to placate the aroused denizen of this fantastic underworld. "Countless red papers, baring sacred hieroglyphics, were burned and cast heavenward to please the angry gods, which seemed bent upon their destruction," wrote Chinatown historian Erica Y. Z. Pan. "Holes were dug in the ground and flaming papers buried in the hope of mollifying the dragon."

Charles Banks wrote that buildings "shaken by the quake, cracked, then toppled over in ruins, burying in the huge piles of debris scores of Chinese. The ornate Joss Houses were the first to fall. Because of their flimsy construction, and the ever-present fires burning therein to placate the gods, they were reduced to ruins and ashes. With the sounding of gongs, the blare of brass, the squeaking of reed instruments, the shrieks of the panic-stricken, the shouts of the maddened populace, the roar of the consuming flames, the groans of the wounded and the moans of the dying, pandemonium reigned, striking terror to every heart and blanching every face with emotions of horror and despair."

W. W. Overton, a visitor from Los Angeles, wrote, "From this place I saw hundreds of crazed yellow men flee. In their arms they bore opium pipes, money bags, silks and children. Beside them ran the trousered women and some hobbled painfully. (It was Chinese custom to tightly bind their feet.) These were the men and women of the surface. Far beneath the street levels in those cellars and passageways were other lives. Women, who never saw the day from their darkened prisons, and their blinking jailors were caught and eaten by the flames."

Fifteen-year-old Hugh Kwong Liang, who was born in San Francisco, at first felt that Chinatown was in no danger of the fire. A large playground above Kearny Street formed a barrier that seemed likely to stop the advance of the flames. But the wind was so strong that the fire swept beyond it. Many years later, Liang wrote, "There was nothing I could do but take courage to carry on and follow the crowd of refugees up over the hills away from Chinatown to face the fate awaiting us."

Looking back from Nob Hill, he saw the building where he'd been born on Washington Street burn. But in the midst of the disaster, he found "a modern miracle" in St. Mary's Church. Defying quake and fire, it remained erect.

"The fire kept coming closer," Liang recalled. "I could hear the continued dynamiting of buildings from distant parts of the city. There was no food or water even though I didn't feel hungry. What was I to do? Oh yes, carry on and on! So I turned away from my dear old Chinatown for the last time and joined the slow march with the other refugees. Presently, city officials directing the refugees march approached us and told us to proceed toward the open grounds at the Presidio Army Post."

Other displaced Chinese made their way to the open spaces of Golden Gate Park and to the area west of Van Ness Avenue that had been saved from the fire. Thousands of others rushed to the waterfront and eventually crossed the bay to Oakland. So many would arrive that, on April 27, an editorial in the *Oakland Herald* complained, "One of the evils springing from the late disaster to San Francisco, one that menaces Oakland exceedingly, but that seems to have escaped attention, is the great influx of Chinese into this city from San Francisco. Not only have they pushed outward the limits of Oakland's heretofore constricted and insignificant Chinatown, but they have settled themselves in large colonies throughout the residence parts of this city, bringing with them their vices and filth."

The editorial continued in a racist rant about the "Mongolians" and "Celestials" who "shuffle in and out" for a reason that "one familiar with their life can easily conjecture." They left members of Oakland's "most exclusive society up in arms." The editorial went on to say, "That opium smoking is going on in Chinatown to a greatly increased extent is known to all familiar with the district. That fan tan and pi glow [gambling games] are being played nightly by hundreds is also certain. These vices have white patrons as well as yellow. Hundreds of Caucasian worshipers at the shrine of the black smoke have been forced to come to Oakland by the fire, and now depend for the satisfaction of their abnormal and vicious appetite upon the Chinese of Oakland. These 'hop heads' are to be seen in droves about the fringe of Chinatown."

Noting that "Chinatown itself has spread from a small affair to a quarter now inhabited by thousands," the newspaper saw the Chinese throwing out "tentacles, taking in more and more houses and streets." White families, it said, "are moving away, unwilling to be surrounded by the degradation, the filth, and the vice that Chinatown means."

Because many of the Chinese refugees occupied a lot owned by the government of China–the former location of the Chinese Consulate and which was to be the site of a new building–a delegation of Chinese diplomats met with California Governor George Pardee to call to his attention a report that Oakland's authorities planned to remove the squatters. China's Vice-Consul General, O Yang King, reminded Pardee, "America is a free country, and every man has a right to occupy land which he owns provided that he makes no nuisance."

The *Chronicle* noted that a plan to relocate Chinese refugees was also afoot in San Francisco. The paper reported on April 25, "The big fire has obliterated Chinatown from San Francisco forever. Mayor Schmitz informed Chief of Police Dinan that all of the Chinese now in the city would be collected and placed in Fontana's warehouses, near Fort Mason, and that Chinatown would be relocated. "All Chinese who have left the city, and who return later," the *Chronicle* reported, "will be concentrated at the new points."

The question of Chinatown's future location was the subject of "animated discussion" at a meeting of Mayor Schmitz's committee of civic leaders on April 26. The chairman of a sub-committee on Chinese resettlement, Dr. Thomas Filben, a Methodist minister, reported that several blocks of vacant land at the foot of Van Ness Avenue had been prepared "under the sanction of federal authorities for the temporary accommodation of all the Chinese in the city." Noting that "adequate sanitary arrangements had been provided, and that the camp was well equipped in all respects for the comfort of the Chinese," he suggested civil and military authorities "proceed at once to gather all the Chinese and establish them in one colony in that location."

At this point, businessman and former mayor James D. Phelan objected "strenuously." He declared that the Van Ness camp was intended to be "temporary" and that any attempt to dislodge the Chinese would be "extremely difficult." He feared property owners in the area would find it "extremely profitable" to keep the Chinese in the area. Phelan preferred moving the refugees to Hunter's Point. On the southern extremity of the city on the bay shore of San Mateo County, it was several miles from the old Chinatown.

Phelan found an ally in Abraham Ruef. The "sole purpose in establishing the temporary camp at the foot of Van Ness Avenue," Ruef said, "was to get all of the Chinese together so that they might be moved more advantageously to permanent quarters when secured." Unsaid was that Ruef and other men with real estate interests had their eyes set on what they considered to be a better use for the property that had been Chinatown.

Attorney Garrett McEnerney gave the argument a legal twist. He said, "I think it will prove difficult for the Chinese to get building permits from the mayor and the Board of Public Works for the erection of any permanent structures at the foot of Van Ness Avenue." He was so confident about this, he said, he was prepared to "buy a long pool" [bet] on it.

But businessman Gavin McNab pointed out that moving the Chinese would deprive San Francisco's treasury of property and poll taxes when the city would need them to help meet the costs of rebuilding. Knowing that Chinatown had been a popular tourist attraction, he added that the city could not afford "to entertain an Oriental city just outside its boundaries."

The committee meeting ended with the adoption of a plan to "gather all Chinese" into a temporary camp at North Beach while another committee studied the subject of a "permanent location of the Chinese quarter." Appointed to the committee were Ruef, Phelan, and Dr. Filben.

Eight days later, the *Examiner* reported, "The white persons and Chinese who are debating the position of a permanent Chinatown away from the old district have as yet come to no agreement." The reason was explained in the next paragraph. It noted that on May 2, Chung Hsi, the Chinese Consul, and O Wyang King, Vice-Consul, had toured outlying districts with Abraham Ruef and found Hunter's Point and other prospective sites unsatisfactory. Hsi also expressed "desires" that the Chinese population of San Francisco "be treated with the same consideration and courtesy accorded Caucasians."

With overtones of racism, the plight and future of the Chinese and Chinatown had by this time become a matter with international consequences. Concerns about the situation had been called to the attention of the U.S. government directly by the Empress-Dowager of China. At stake was not only where the Chinese of San Francisco would be settled, but whether the city could maintain its role as the Golden Gate for American trade with the rich markets of the Far East. In the end, the issue would be decided by economics, combined with embarrassment over San Francisco being portrayed around the world as a haven for racists. The issue of a white land-grab was also settled when Abraham Ruef concluded that the city could claim no legal basis for taking over Chinese property.

Although it seemed that what the white population of the city had wanted for fifty years–to be rid of the Chinese–had been accomplished in seconds by the fire, the conflagration also destroyed immigration records and vital statistics at City Hall. As a result, many Chinese were able to claim American citizenship and not be disputed. Citizenship allowed them to bring their children and families from China in what whites saw as a wave of "paper sons and paper daughters," who also claimed citizenship.

Meanwhile, a wealthy businessman named Look Tin Eli developed his own plan to rebuild Chinatown at its original location. He obtained a loan from Hong Kong and designed the new Chinatown to be more emphatically "Oriental," in order to draw tourists. The result, noted a later historian, was a new Chinatown "looking like a stage-set China that does not exist."

Fifteen

✿

BEYOND ALL PRAISE

✿

*A*S REPORTS OF THE DISASTER IN SAN Francisco flowed to the opposite side of the continent, President Theodore Roosevelt was already calculating what aid would be needed from the federal government once the fire was out.

The logistical problem of providing assistance to the stricken city was complicated by Roosevelt's knowledge that he would have to deal with an elected leader who embodied the kind of political corruption that Roosevelt had been fighting against his entire public life. He was an advocate of imposing federal restraints on the political influence of the nation's railroads; yet, the Southern Pacific Railroad controlled Mayor Schmitz and everyone else in San Franciscan and Californian politics. Its president, Edward H. Harriman, and corporate friends had raised five million dollars in an effort to defeat Roosevelt in the 1904 election.

Roosevelt was also aware that Abraham Ruef was the chief political fixer of the Southern Pacific Railroad. Ruef was the man who had engineered Schmitz's political rise, and had personally profited from the corruption of Schmitz's administration. Yet these were the individuals in charge of dealing with the disaster and would also be in control of relief, recovery, and reconstruction. Schmitz had made his intentions clear in a telegram to Roosevelt. Sent on Saturday, April 21, it said, "We are determined to restore to the nation its chief port on the Pacific."

Determined to keep Mayor Schmitz and his hand-picked disaster committee from getting their hands on relief money and materials, Roosevelt announced that everything was to be handled by the Red Cross under the supervision of Secretary of Commerce Victor H. Metcalf. The Red Cross agent in San Francisco would be Dr. Edward Devine. All federal relief money and funds contributed by the public would be given to a finance committee whose chairman was to be a man whose honesty Roosevelt felt no need to question. He named former Mayor James Phelan, the man who had spearheaded the probe of corruption in Schmitz's government.

With these safeguards in place, Roosevelt issued this proclamation:

TO THE PUBLIC:—When the news of the dreadful disaster at San Francisco first came it was necessary to take immediate steps to provide in some way for the receipt and distribution of the sums of money which at once poured in for the relief of the people of San Francisco. At the moment no one could foretell how soon it would be possible for the people of San Francisco themselves to organize to tide over the interval the American National Red Cross Association was designated to receive and distribute funds.

But the people of San Francisco, with an energy and self-reliant courage, a cool resourcefulness and a capacity for organization and orderly endeavor which are beyond all praise, have already met the need, through committees appointed by the mayor of the city, ex-Mayor James D. Phelan being the chairman of the finance committee. The work of these committees has been astonishing in its range, promptness and efficiency.... Thanks to their efforts, no individual is now suffering for food, water or temporary shelter. This work has been done with the minimum of waste and under conditions which would have appalled men less trained in business methods, endowed with less ability, or inspired with any but the highest motives of humanity and helpfulness.

While policing of the city and care of refugee camps and hospitals was put in the hands of the Army, Roosevelt was concerned about damage done to coastal defenses. After a survey of the installations, the *Examiner* reported on April 24, 1906, "The big fortifications at the entrance to the Golden Gate did not escape serious injury during the great shakeup. The full extent of the injury is as yet unknown, for nothing but a survey by the engineering corps can disclose the full extent of the damage. At Lime Point the emplacements of the big guns have been cracked and twisted. Conditions are said to be equally as bad at the fortifications of old Fort Point. As it is now, the great 13-inch guns on both sides of the gate, constituting the main defense are practically useless."

Two days later, Roosevelt's concerns were somewhat allayed by Secretary of Commerce and Labor Victor Metcalf. Also Roosevelt's personal representative in San Francisco, he said in a long telegram, "The fortifications are practically uninjured. Considerable damage was done to the military buildings at the Presidio and Angel Island. Reports indicate there was no damage to the buildings on Alcatraz Island. The army warehouses in the city were entirely destroyed."

Because San Francisco was the main military shipping point to the Philippines, the Army, Navy, and Marine Corps, based at Manila and elsewhere in the islands, lost millions of dollars worth of supplies to the quake and fire. This news was especially worrisome to Roosevelt. He feared a growing menace to American territorial and commercial interests in the Pacific from an increasingly bellicose Japan, on the issue of American restrictions of Japanese immigration to the United States. This was of particular worry to a group of San Francisco's labor leaders. Known as The Japanese and Korean Exclusion League, they had organized in 1905 to pressure Congress to reject a bill admitting anyone from China who claimed to be a student, merchant, or traveler. They wanted to expand an existing law that limited Chinese immigration in order to prevent a fresh "Asiatic coolie invasion." They warned that if the proposed bill had become law, it would have "thrown down the bars and admitted every Chinaman to our shores who desires to come here."

The group contended that "the Japanese coolie is even a greater menace to the existence of the white race [and] to the progress and prosperity of our country than is the Chinese coolie." It warned, "The great calamity which befell San Francisco will furnish the Orient with lurid tales of opportunity for employment and profit. California, the land of fabulous wealth, revenue and mountains of gold, and San Francisco with its wonderful images will be exploited before the ignorant coolies until they come in ship loads like an endless swarm of rats. Do not for a moment think that the Japanese will keep away on account of the earthquakes. They are raised on earthquakes in Japan, and the earthquake will only make the Nipponese coolies feel more at home in California. Great as the recent catastrophe has been, let us take care lest we encounter a greater one. We can withstand the earthquake. We can survive the fire. As long as California is white man's country, it will remain one of the grandest and best states in the Union, but the moment the Golden State is subjected to an unlimited Asiatic coolie invasion there will be no more California."

Mayor Schmitz supported this view. The former member of a musicians' union, and the first labor leader to be elected to office in the United States, assured the Pacific Wrecking Company that he "would not countenance importation or use of coolie labor in San Francisco," nor would he "favor competition of cheap labor against American white labor."

Consequently, he did not interfere when the Pacific Trades Council ordered its members not to work on buildings on sites that had been cleared or prepared by "Asiatic labor."

While there was nothing Roosevelt could do to interfere with the discrimination against Asian laborers in San Francisco, he found himself forced to take action after San Francisco's Board of Education announced that Japanese children could not go to school with whites, but must attend schools for Japanese students only. Learning of this new policy, the Japanese government directed its ambassador in Washington to inform the United States government that the segregation order "had produced among all classes of people in Japan a feeling of profound disappointment and sorrow," and that it expected the order to be reversed.

Roosevelt denounced the policy as "wickedly absurd," and promised Japan to take up the matter in his next message to Congress. Meanwhile, he delegated the crisis to Victor Metcalf, and vowed to "exert all the power I have under the Constitution to protect the rights of the Japanese who are here." The *Sacramento Union* retorted with an allusion to Roosevelt's famous policy to speak softly but carry a big stick. The newspaper said, "Not even the big stick is big enough to compel the people of California to do a thing which they have a fixed determination not to do."

With a wary eye on the Japanese navy, Roosevelt was unwilling to be drawn into a war over the issue of Japanese school children when he felt the United States fleet was not strong enough to prevail. After lengthy negotiations, a "Gentlemen's Agreement" was reached in which the segregation order would be rescinded, Japan would not issue passports to the mainland of the United States, and immigration of Japanese from Hawaii would be restricted.

Roosevelt complained, "Nothing during my presidency has given me more concern than these troubles." Still worried about Japan in the summer of 1907, he asked the joint Army and Navy Board to send him their plans in the event of a war with Japan, then directed the Navy to have battleships in the Pacific by October. He masked his purpose by calling the deployment of the ships "a practice cruise."

In dealing with an outpouring of offers of aid from world governments, Roosevelt said he and the American people were grateful, but the contributions were declined. Although he did not reply that the United States was able to take care of itself, his message was clear. Among the financial aid that Roosevelt declined was 100,000 taels from the Dowager-Empress of China, which was offered in an "Imperial Decree on the 30th Day of the Third Moon."

Roosevelt acted with Metcalf's assurance that the situation in San Francisco was well in hand. He reported that the "efforts of the Mayor and municipal officials of the Citizens' Committee, and of the regular army and the State Guard of California have been practically as efficient as though the separate authorities were under one head. Neither friction nor reflections have at any time appeared, and the work of relief has proceeded harmoniously, continuously and efficiently."

Sixteen

✦

LAST STAND

✦

OR THREE LONG DAYS, FIRE HAD SWEPT across the city. Unchecked because of the lack of water, pushed by wind off the bay, and undaunted by dynamite, the flames had consumed all in their path on the flat expanse of South of Market from the ferry docks to City Hall and beyond. It tore through Chinatown, and then up Telegraph Hill, Russian Hill, and Nob Hill to the divide of Van Ness Avenue past which lay the Western Addition. To clothier Frederick H. Collins it was "a gray and black graveyard."

Within minutes of the first jolt of the earthquake at 5:13 on Wednesday morning, the fire department responded to reports of small fires resulting from burning coals spilling from kitchen stoves, overturned heaters fueled by coal oil, and broken electrical wires. Engine Co. 2 had rushed to a rooming house across from Union Square called "The Geary." The initial call for Engine Co. 4 was directly across Howard Street from the fire station to a Chinese laundry. Engine Co. 6 was summoned to a fire in a bakery on Sixth Street between Howard and Folsom, which quickly merged with a blaze on Howard Street. One fire at the San Francisco Gas and Electric Company (SFG&E), caused by a fallen smokestack that spread to envelop the Mission Opera House, Palace Hotel, and the *Call* building, also melded with the Howard Street fire as the blaze moved east and west to link with the Hayes Valley "Ham and Eggs" fire.

Very quickly, there were so many blazes going that the fire department could not keep up; the phrase in official reports was "Not attended by SFFD." Among those the department could not respond to was a blaze at the California Fireworks factory at Front and Sacramento that merged with one on Davis Street and marched westward toward Chinatown and up Nob Hill. Two fires listed as "not attended" were "suppressed" by the occupants of 2007 Devisadero Street and a home at 728 Montgomery Street, in which fire had ignited when boxes of non-safety matches fell from shelves to floors. An unattended fire in a collapsed home on Natoma Street combined with the SFG&E fire.

The reality facing the fire fighters on the date that chief engineer Patrick H. Shaughnessy called "the memorial 18th of April" was that the SFFD was also a quake victim. "The temblor having played havoc with our entire fire alarm system," noted Shaughnessy, "not an alarm bell rang to warn the department that fires were raging all over the city." When firemen responded, he continued, "hydrant after hydrant was tested and not a drop of water was to be found."

Following the decision to check the advance of the fire by blowing up buildings to create a firebreak, the explosive supplied to firemen and soldiers was of powder form. When it was ignited, the explosion threw off sparks that set splintered wood ablaze. These were cited in the official reports as "not original fires." When black powder was replaced by stick dynamite, there were "splendid results," in which there was no combustion.

Around five o'clock in the morning on April 20, it appeared that the battle to halt the fire at the east side of Van Ness Avenue had succeeded. General Funston signaled the War Department, "Fire is making no progress west of Van Ness." Noting that a wind of "considerable force" was beginning, he held out no hope for saving "all of that part of the city east of Van Ness and north of the bay," but believed that Fort Mason (Funston's headquarters) could be saved.

Of the moment when salvation appeared at hand, a policeman recalled, "Men, women, and children were thanking God that the disaster that had rendered them homeless and penniless was ended at last."

Then the Viavi Building on the northeast corner of Van Ness and Vallejo Street went up with a huge explosion. Flaming debris went flying. Someone yelled, "For God's sake! What did they do that for?"

The restarted fire threatened to sweep from Van Ness down into the Western Addition, and eat its way through Russian Hill and onward to the North Beach district and nearby Fort Mason. Fanned by strong winds from the northwest, it moved quickly, preceded by a wave of panicked residents who found themselves caught between a fire on three sides and the bay on the north.

As about twenty thousand refugees faced what seemed to be a choice between certain incineration and the chance that they might drown by leaping into the water, General Funston took on the role of admiral. The rescue armada, formed with every kind of boat from Army tugs and Navy craft to rowboats and fishing vessels, and manned by soldiers, sailors, firemen, and civilian volunteers, converged on Meiggs and Fisherman's Wharves. From midnight until dawn, wrote an observer, the men were "fighting fire as never fire had been fought before." The tugs aimed "immense streams of water onto the flames of burning factories, warehouses, and sheds." Still, hundreds of people who could not scramble onto a boat or would not risk leaping into the water perished.

Eight-year-old DeWitt C. Baldwin had looked with awe at "a powerful blaze consuming everything before it." He watched it beyond Mission Street from the back stairs of the three-story building that was home to him, an older sister, a baby sister, a music-loving mother who insisted that he learn the piano, and his father, an officer of the United Railroads of San Francisco. DeWitt recalled that as the fire grew, he began to think of "the destructive power of fire and realized that fire was more destructive to man and his environment than any cause I had known." As it came nearer to his home, he thought, "This is getting serious."

Ordered to evacuate and "find shelter in the hills," the Baldwins became part of a vast assemblage in which contemporary chronicler of the quake Charles Morris found "no caste, no distinction of rich and poor, social lines had been obliterated by the common misfortune, and the late owners of property and wealth were glad to camp by the side of the day laborer." He also found "unspeakable chaos" in a system, "or lack of system, of registration and location" that was supposed to help refugees locate relatives and friends.

Billboards, tree trunks, posts, and sides of wagons and automobiles became festooned with desperate messages scrawled on scraps of paper, business cards, stationery, and anything else that could be written on. They begged for information ("I am looking for I. E. Hall") or gave it ("Sue, Harry and Will Sollenberger all safe. Call at No. 250 Twenty-seventh Avenue").

Tents were often given names, either of the occupants, former addresses, or expressions of refugee-camp humor, including "Camp Thankful," "Camp Glory," and "Camp Hell." Morris wrote, "To those who made an inspection of the situation a few days after the earthquake, the hills and beaches of San Francisco looked like an immense tented city. Golden Gate Park looked like one vast campaign ground. It is said that fully 100,000 persons, rich and poor alike, sought refuge in Golden Gate Park alone, and 200,000 more homeless ones located at the other places of refuge."

Yet, amid all this chaos, life went on. Weddings that were to take place at a future date were moved up, ministers were located, and the ceremonies conducted on the spot. There were also births, including five on one night in Golden Gate Park.

One of the saddest results of the earthquake and fire was the large number of children who had been either orphaned or separated from parents. So many children and babies showed up in the care of strangers who had fled on trains from Oakland to Salem, Oregon, that the state's governor, George E. Chamberlain, sent a message to California Governor George Pardee asking, "Can they not be gathered together at Oakland and kept together for subsequent identification? As it is, they will be forever lost to their parents."

William Randolph Hearst's *Examiner* reported a resolution to this crisis. It noted that Pardee referred the matter to the Oakland relief committee. That group in turn appointed a committee of one, the Reverend B. Fay Mills, to "make arrangements." The article continued, "Mr. Mills conferred with Colonel French of the Salvation Army, and the result of their efforts was the founding of Beulah Park, where the Salvation Army's rescue home is situated, a camp, financed by W. R. Hearst and to be known as the 'W. R. Hearst Reunion Camp for Children.' "

Hearst had jumped into his hometown's crisis with his usual dramatic flair. In addition to organizing the previously mentioned relief trains, he had arranged relief fund-raising through charity bazaars and theatrical benefits in New York City. In a hurried trip to the nation's capital, he saw that a bill was introduced to Congress for rebuilding public structures in San Francisco. He then headed west, as noted earlier, with $200,000 raised by the other newspapers in his empire.

To assist employees of the *Examiner*, he ordered a pay-boost of a dollar a day, but only until they were again on their feet financially. When their boss arrived, the paper was still operating in Oakland. Eager to have the newspaper functioning on its own, he sought to buy new presses. The manufacturers told him that they were unable to deliver them on such short notice, but he learned of a press that had been recently bought by a paper in Salt Lake City. He purchased it for twice the price and arranged for shipment to San Francisco.

Among the *Examiner* stories was one headlined:

ORPHANS ARE DRIVEN FROM THEIR SHELTER

Noting that San Francisco "had more than a score of institutions devoted to the housing and care of children," the story reported that "in the whole record of their crumbling walls and showers of plaster only one life was lost—that of an infant in the Alexander maternity cottage."

The article continued, "To any one viewing the remains of the large and supposedly substantial buildings which housed the orphans of San Francisco it seems miraculous that many lives were not crushed out. Roofs tumbled in, furniture was shattered, window glass flew in all directions and panics among the children resulted, yet all were saved and have since been removed to places which appear to offer greater safety than the buildings which remain in this city."

The *Examiner* reporter found an inspiring angle to include in his story. "Many cases of child heroism can be told," the story began. "One case is reported at the Kip orphanage of a fifteen-year-old boy who, in the midst of the excitement, climbed a water-pipe and re-entered the crumbling building to get his younger brother a pair of pants." Another boy named Connelly "had to be dragged away from his work of throwing quilts and cots out of windows."

Young Lloyd Head, member of the Theodore Roosevelt Boys' Club in the 1200 block of Treat Avenue, found the earthquake and fire an adventure. He admitted that as he held onto the side of his bed when it began shaking, he was so scared he "couldn't even yell." Afterwards, he ran into his parents' bedroom, shared with Lloyd's baby sister. For the club's newsletter, "Our Junior Citizens," published on July 28, 1906, he wrote, "My father didn't seem scared very much, but I guess he was, all the same, and so were all of us except the baby; she just sat up in bed and didn't even cry, but I'll bet she thought it was kind of funny whenever we heard a rumble and we all piled into the back yard as fast as we could."

Uncertain of the stability of their house, the Head family prepared to find safety in an open space on one of the hills. They made tents by sewing sacks together and settled into the backyard. "I believe we should have enjoyed our camping out," Lloyd wrote, "but as it was it was anything but pleasant. There was no water and the noise of buildings being blown up continually startled us."

But seventy-four hours after the start of the worst earthquake in San Francisco's history, and the greatest ever felt in the United States, the dynamiting stopped. At 7:15 A.M., on Saturday, April 21, 1906, the fire was declared out.

Lieutenant Frederick Freeman of the U.S. Navy had no doubt in his mind that if he'd had "fresh men" available to fight the fire on the docks on Friday morning, "more property would have been saved, as my men were thoroughly exhausted from that time on and could not work with stamina." To James Hopper of the *Call*, the men were an inspiration. "When they dropped exhausted, in the gutters," he said, "somebody would always be there to pull them to their feet and help them carry on. Their helmets were baked to their heads and their turn–out rig was peeling off their backs."

Burned out in an area of four square miles were more than twenty-eight thousand buildings, mostly wooden structures. Total property damage was an estimated $400 million, with three-fourths of that sum attributed to the fire.

As if Mother Nature felt not enough suffering had been inflicted during the previous three days, Sunday, April 22, brought heavy rain.

Seventeen

THE GOVERNOR, THE MAYOR, AND THE GENERALS

MPEDED BY DAMAGED ROADBED ON THE railway between Sacramento and San Francisco, Governor George Pardee was not able to reach Oakland until two in the morning on April 19. Born in San Francisco in 1857, but raised in Oakland, he'd followed in his father's footsteps by becoming a doctor and politician. He specialized in diseases of the eye and ear, and loved cigars, straw hats, and Florida Water cologne. He served on Oakland's Board of Health and City Council and later as mayor. In addition to keeping an open door as governor, he kept his medical bag on the hall table of the governor's mansion in case he needed to make a house call.

A compromise between two factions of the Republican Party as candidate for Governor of California in the election of 1902, he'd found himself like the man in a circus high-wire act. His challenge as governor was to keep his balance between so-called "Railroad Republicans" with powerful ties to the state's dominant economic force, the Southern Pacific Railway, and a group of reformers in the style of Theodore Roosevelt. Referred to as "the man in the middle," Pardee had maintained a policy of keeping his office door open while meeting with members of one group or another.

Establishing headquarters in the office of Oakland's mayor, Frank Mott, on April 19, Pardee declared a three-day business holiday (Thursday, Friday, and Saturday), began sending telegrams asking for emergency aid from the federal government, and called out the National Guard (state militia). Depending on whom he asked, the people in charge in San Francisco were either Mayor Schmitz and his citizens' committee, or the U.S. Army, under command of Brigadier General Frederick Funston, not Major General Greely, as Pardee had expected.

Adolphus Washington Greely missed the quake because he was in Chicago for his daughter's wedding, and he would not return to the city until Sunday, April 22. A soldier since 1861, he'd enlisted at age 17 in the Nineteenth Massachusetts Volunteer Infantry and had engaged in some of the bloodiest fighting of the Civil War. Shot in the face at the Battle of Antietam, he concealed a disfiguring scar with a lavishly bushy beard. He was commissioned as a second lieutenant in the regular army following the war and detailed to the Signal Corps, where he'd learned telegraphy, helped organize the U.S. Weather Bureau, and became known as an adept meteorologist. After participating in the construction of telegraph lines on the frontier, he volunteered to lead a weather expedition to the Arctic in 1881 and spent three years on Ellesmere Island near the North Pole. Awarded the Founder's Medal of the Royal Geographical Society of London and the Roquette Medal of the *Société de Géographie* of Paris, he was also named Chief Signal Officer of the U.S. Army by President Grover Cleveland with rank of brigadier general. This gave Greely the distinction of being the first volunteer private soldier of the Civil War to become a general in the regular army. After directing the Signal Corps in the Spanish-American War, he represented the United States at the International Wireless Telegraph Congress in Berlin in 1903. As commander of the Northern Division of the Army in 1905, he negotiated an end to a rebellion by Ute Indians. Promoted to Major General, he was placed in command of the Pacific Division just two months before the earthquake. When

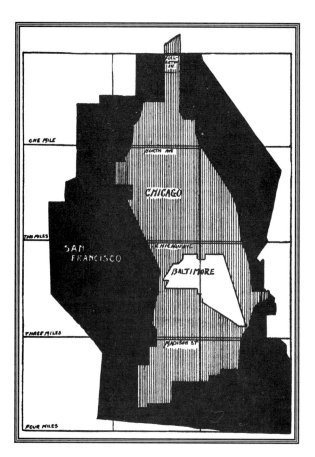

A comparative area of burned districts of Baltimore, Chicago, and San Francisco. The loss due to fire in San Francisco was about $350,000,000.

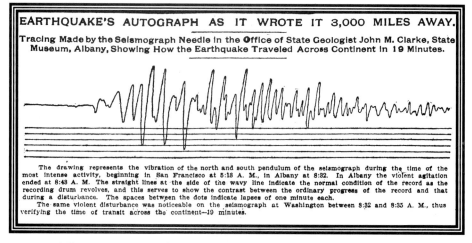

This seismograph of the earthquake published in The New York Times *on April 19, 1906 showed that the shock was registered in New York nineteen minutes later.*

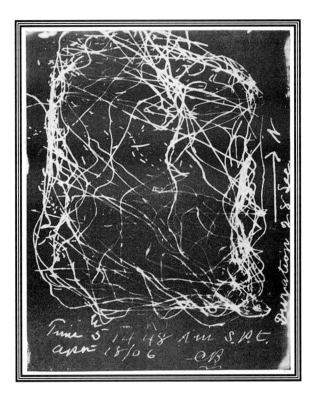

A signature of the earthquake which occurred on April 18, 1906.

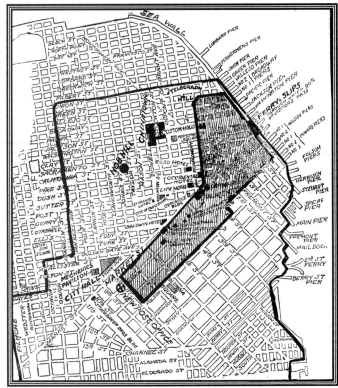

A map of the area destroyed by the fire. The shaded area shows the extent of the fire on the first day. The black line indicates how far the flames reached by day two.

Chief of Police Jeremiah Dinan.

OVER 500 DEAD, $200,000,000 LOST IN SAN FRANCISCO EARTHQUAKE

Nearly Half the City Is in Ruins and 50,000 Are Homeless.

WATER SUPPLY FAILS AND DYNAMITE IS USED IN VAIN

Great Buildings Consumed Before Helpless Firemen—Federal Troops and Militia Guard the City, With Orders to Shoot Down Thieves—Citizens Roused in Early Morning by Great Convulsion and Hundreds Caught by Falling Walls.

SAN FRANCISCO, April 18.—Earthquake and fire to-day have put nearly half of San Francisco in ruins. About 500 persons have been killed, a thousand injured, and the property loss will exceed $200,000,000.

Fifty thousand people are homeless and destitute, and all day long streams of people have been fleeing from the stricken districts to places of safety.

It was 5:13 this morning when a terrific earthquake shock shook the whole city and surrounding country. One shock apparently lasted two minutes, and there was almost immediate collapse of flimsy structures all over the city.

The water supply was cut off, and when fires started in various sections there was nothing to do but let the buildings burn. Telegraph and telephone communication was cut off for a time.

The Western Union was put completely out of business and the Postal Company was the only one that managed the roof sliding into the courtyard, and the smaller towers tumbling down. The great dome was moved, but did not fall.

The new Post Office, one of the finest in the United States, was badly shattered.

The Valencia Hotel, a four-story wooden building, sank into the basement, a pile of splintered timbers, under which were pinned many dead and dying occupants of the house. The basement was full of water, and some of the helpless victims were drowned.

Fires Start in Many Places.

Scarcely had the earth ceased to shake when fires started simultaneously in many places. The Fire Department promptly responded to the first calls for aid, but it was found that the water mains had been rendered useless by the underground movement.

Fanned by a light breeze, the flames quickly spread, and soon many blocks were seen to be doomed. Then dynamite was resorted to, and the sound of frequent explosions added to the terror of the people. These efforts to stay the progress of the fire, however, proved futile.

The south side of Market Street,

This article appeared as the front-page story of
The New York Times, *April 19, 1906.*

PROCLAMATION
BY THE MAYOR

The Federal Troops, the members of the Regular Police Force and all Special Police Officers have been authorized by me to KILL any and all persons found engaged in Looting or in the Commission of Any Other Crime.

I have directed all the Gas and Electric Lighting Co.'s not to turn on Gas or Electricity until I order them to do so. You may therefore expect the city to remain in darkness for an indefinite time.

I request all citizens to remain at home from darkness until daylight every night until order is restored.

I WARN all Citizens of the danger of fire from Damaged or Destroyed Chimneys, Broken or Leaking Gas Pipes or Fixtures, or any like cause.

E. E. SCHMITZ, Mayor

Dated, April 18, 1906.

ALTVATER PRINT, MISSION AND 220

*Proclamation made by
Mayor E. E. Schmitz
to the citizens of
San Francisco.*

*Mayor of
San Francisco,
Eugene E. Schmitz.*

The remains of William Randolph Hearst's
Examiner *building after the earthquake.*

Newspaper publisher William Randolph Hearst, owner of the San Francisco Examiner, *which was destroyed in the fire.*

A SECTION OF EAST STREET ON THE WATERFRONT WHERE THE FIRE STARTED.

THE SAME HOUSES ON EAST STREET FIFTEEN MINUTES LATER.

This page from a special issue of Collier's magazine showed a section of East Street when the fire started and fifteen minutes later.

A view of Nob Hill from Sutter Street and Grant Avenue before the fire.

A view of Nob Hill from St. Mary's Cathedral after the fire.
Van Ness Avenue bread line appears in the foreground.

An observatory located on Strawberry Hill in Golden Gate Park, San Francisco, after having been damaged by the earthquake.

A view of Turk and Market Streets, San Francisco, after the fire.

Smoke billows rise above the Market Street business district.

View near Turk and Market St.

The burning of San Francisco, April 18. View from St. Francis Hotel.
Library of Congress [DLC/PP-1906:42912]

View near Turk and Market Street.
Library of Congress [DLC/PP-1906:42933]

Fire on Fifth Street about the United States Mint.

The Mint in San Francisco withstood both earthquake and fire with scarcely any damage.

The Valencia Street Hotel shown before the earthquake.
Copyright 1906. Chas. Perry. Used by Permission.

Thirty people were killed in the destruction of the Valencia Street Four-Story Hotel.

The new post office in San Francisco did not suspend business except for a few hours to fight fire. The Grant Building is shown at left.

The Jefferson Square camp of refugees.

After having been destroyed by fire, the Grand Opera House lay in ruins.

The buckling of the earth was a result of the earthquake on Mission Street opposite the post office.

Houses saved from the fire on Russian Hill.

*This severe break in the street near the waterfront
was caused by the earthquake.*

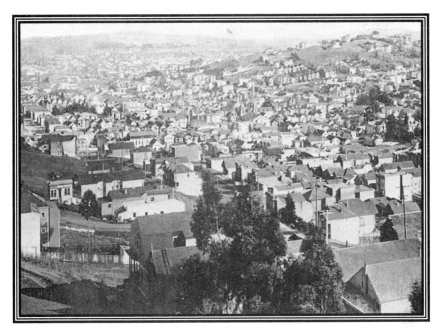

*A view from Ashbury Heights showing the unburned
portion of the Mission District after the fire.*

*A view of the burning of the Mission District, as
seen from Market Street, near Dolores Street.*

Copyright 1906. A. Blumberg, Cal. Used by permission.

The Kohl Building on California and Montgomery Streets withstood both fire and earthquake and was used as the headquarters by the commanding officers of the military.

The Lincoln School on Fifth Street was damaged by fire.

People waiting in a bread line on Folsom Street, San Francisco.

*A view of Capp Street, near Seventeenth, after having
been damaged by the earthquake.*

*The cottages on Golden Gate Avenue, near Hyde Street
were wrecked by the earthquake.*

Looking down Sutter Street, San Francisco, after the fire.

This view down Fell Street shows how closely people clung to their homes, only leaving when fire was a few doors away.

Copyright, 1906, by A. Blumberg.

View from the bay as the city burns on the morning of April 18, 1906.
Used by Permission

People who had escaped the fire rested in Union Square.
All buildings shown here afterwards burned.

The break in the street on Van Ness Avenue, near Vallejo Street, was
caused by the earthquake. Water mains were also broken here.

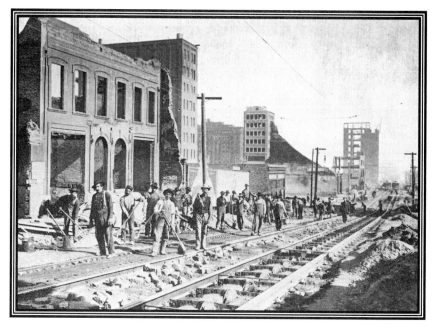

Shown here are men repairing the tracks on Sutter Street after the fire. The line was later changed from cable to electric.

A view from Ashbury Heights of the Sunset District, which went unharmed by fire or earthquake.

The Old Mission Dolores was unhurt by earthquake or fire.

This shot, taken in November of 1906, shows the four blocks from Sixteenth to Twentieth Streets, which were rebuilt after the fire.

The north side Market Street, between Jones and Larkin, was rebuilt after the fire, as shown in this portion of a photograph taken in November of 1906.

*A view of some new buildings on Fillmore Street, the
principal business center, immediately after the fire.*

*The Stanford Library at Stanford University
was damaged by the earthquake.*

*The Wells Fargo Bank Building in Santa Rosa
was destroyed by the earthquake.*

The Hotel Vendome Annex in San Jose was wrecked by the earthquake.

San Francisco's new, six-million-dollar City Hall before the quake.

San Francisco's new, six-million-dollar City Hall after the quake.

View of the ruins in the valley that sweeps from Russian Hill to Telegraph Hill, showing Alcatraz Island in the distance, July 14, 1906.
Library of Congress [LC-USZ62-124174 DLC]

Shown is Refugee Camp No. 13. Thousands of U.S. Army tents were rushed to the city from military posts all over the western half of the United States.

*View of the western addition and the Mission, showing the ruins
of City Hall and St. Ignatius College, August 5, 1906.*
Library of Congress [LC-USZ62-127743 DLC]

Litter-strewn Market Street on the day after the fire was declared out.

What was left of the Tivoli Opera House after the earthquake.

What was left of the popular French restaurant called the Poodle Dog.

he arrived at Fort Mason on April 22, he found that in his absence the distinction between military and civil authority had been blurred. Soldiers and sailors worked as firefighters and often did the job without the aid of the fire department. The Army and Marine Corps also had been forced to take on the job of policing. The state militia, ordered into action by Pardee, further complicated the demarcation of authority. Instead of providing help as keepers of law and order, they had proven to be undisciplined and frequently criminal.

According to a report in the *Chronicle,* about 150 guardsmen spent days looting in Chinatown. Complaints had also been made by merchants and homeowners that rather than protecting property, militiamen had become pillagers and thieves themselves.

While Major General Greely had no doubt that Funston's use of federal forces to maintain law and order had been significant in protecting property and lives, its legality was dubious. Funston had supplanted legitimate civil authority and made himself, in effect, a military dictator, while he told his superiors in Washington that he was carrying out Secretary of War Taft's order that he work in harmony with the mayor and do nothing without Schmitz's approval and cooperation. In truth, Funston had persistently acted on his own to prevent a mayor whom he disliked, and who was facing a probe into public corruption, from using the disaster to rehabilitate his reputation.

Consequently, when Schmitz requested that the Army issue rifles to a thousand "special policemen," Funston was suspicious of Schmitz's motive. He was confident that Secretary of War Taft would not approve of giving weapons to what would be the mayor's personal army, and told Schmitz that he could do so only with the approval of the War Department. Taft, however, had replied not only with approval of the request, but also with an order to "detail some noncommissioned officers to instruct the citizens sworn in to properly use the rifle."

Schmitz then requested that Funston take command of the National Guard stationed in the city. With no desire to take over an undisciplined force that might reflect on the demeanor and reputation of his fellow professionals, the brigadier general who had not flinched at brushing aside the Constitution by imposing military rule now asserted that he had no legal authority to take over state troops. Not wanting to be held accountable for the misdemeanor of militiamen, Schmitz requested that the Citizens' Committee appeal to Governor Pardee to withdraw them. The request included a blatantly hypocritical "note of thanks for the efficient services in maintaining law and order." When Governor Pardee asked General Greely to take over control of the militia, Greely also declined. The result was that Guardsmen remained in the city with no one in state and local government willing to publicly admit that the militia was out of control.

Victor Metcalf, as a result of this political maneuvering, erroneously telegraphed to the White House on April 26, "The efforts of the mayor and municipal officials of the Citizens' Committee, and of the regular army and the State Guard of California have been practically as efficient as though the separate authorities were under one head. Neither friction nor reflections have at any time appeared, and the work of the relief has proceeded harmoniously, continuously and efficiently."

This fabrication extended to state that Schmitz and the Citizens' Committee concurred in Greely commending "in the highest terms the efficient and tireless efforts of General Funston, whose orders and actions utilized and inspired the Army to the most efficient action in staying the progress of the flames, and saving the remnant of the city." Funston deserved the praise, but had frequently acted despite what Schmitz had desired and, in some cases, had countermanded the mayor's orders. But the political reality presented to Roosevelt's man in San Francisco and to elected city and state government officials was that Funston had emerged as a people's hero. Secretary of War Taft could have claimed that Funston had run roughshod over the Constitution and made himself a military dictator worthy of a Caesar, but none of the bewildered, bedraggled, and battered people of San Francisco in Army refugee camps cared.

The mayor, who on the day before the ground moved faced a probe into criminal charges, also was not eager to appear usurped by a brigadier general. Choosing to use what a later generation of politicians would call a "spin," Schmitz asserted that he approved everything that Funston had done. Once the fire was out and Funston's boss was back in town, he decided it was time to assert that the city's true savior had been himself. Consequently, as noted earlier, Schmitz wasted no time in shooting off a telegram to Roosevelt with a promise that he would soon restore to the nation its "chief port on the Pacific."

Concerned that the city's reputation would suffer when the death toll was calculated, Schmitz's administration set the number at 498 and General Greely endorsed that figure. A more reasonable tally proposed in 1972 by the U.S. government was between 700 and 800. But a study of a variety of city records by Gladys Hansen and Emmett Condon in their book *Denial of Disaster* confirmed three thousand deaths and estimated that because so many people could not be accounted for, the correct toll probably was between five and ten thousand.

Schmitz and city officials were not alone in downplaying the extent of the disaster. Joining in the obfuscation was the publicity bureau of the Southern Pacific Railroad. As the state's greatest political and economic power, the company launched a campaign to emphasize the rebuilding of the city. It did so through a company-sponsored magazine called *Sunset*. The man in charge of extolling the wonders of California was the Southern Pacific's general passenger agent, James Hofsburgh, Jr. Determined to dispel "false impressions in the East regarding the recent disaster," he distributed a circular to the state's chambers of commerce to lay out a propaganda effort to counter what he predicted would be "a great many people giving lectures upon the earthquake and fire who, because of the interest attached thereto, will dwell upon the dramatic features of the situation."

He recommended that chambers of commerce "reach every one of these lecturers and get them to make the story complete–that is, not only to represent the vivid details of the catastrophe itself, but to give over at least the latter half of the lecture to views and data showing how quickly and wonderfully San Francisco and California recovered from the effects, and how thoroughly and systematically they began with the work of reconstruction." He proposed that the use of newspapers and magazines could do "more good" than any other medium of publicity.

Hofsburgh advised, "Let the whole idea be that the main thing in connection with the event was the clearing of a pathway to a greater San Francisco and the awakening to an even greater California." He continued:

> You may be able to secure this result, so far as lectures are concerned, by controlling those lecturers who are going into the field on a commercial basis, rather than by sending out lecturers who might be looked upon in some degree as glossers over the real facts. Any attempt to disguise the truth will result in failure, but every effort should be made to bring forth prominently the sunshine that is to follow the storm.
>
> We [Southern Pacific] stand ready to cooperate with you in every way practicable to keep California and San Francisco from being misrepresented by the sensation mongers.
>
> We do not believe in advertising the earthquake. The real calamity was undoubtedly the fire. In press matter [news releases], I would call attention to the small area of the state which was affected by the earthquake and the relatively small results in the way of destruction, and point out the great buildings of the business section of San Francisco and the residence portion of the city that escaped burning as proof that San Francisco did not suffer greatly from the earthquake.

San Franciscans were urged not to speak of the "great earthquake," but of "the fire."

Efforts were taken not only to persuade geologists not to give out data on the quake, but to allay fears of future ones. Father Ricard, a professor of geology at the University of Santa Clara, wrote to the *San Jose Mercury*:

> The earthquake period is gone. Once the pent up forces of nature have had a vent, nothing of a serious nature need be apprehended. At the most a succession of minor shocks may be felt and that's all. It is unreasonable, therefore, for people to continue in dread of a new destructive temblor. People should fearlessly go to work and repair mischief done and sleep quietly at night anywhere at all, especially in wooden frame. Never mind foreboders of evil; they do not know what they are talking about. Seismonetry is in its infancy and those therefore who venture out with predictions of future earthquakes when the main shock has taken place ought to be arrested as disturbers of the peace.

All of this was a case of whistling past the graveyard and locking the barn door after the horse was stolen. Days after the fire was out, the nation was flooded with picture postcards portraying quake-wrecked buildings. Within months, books appeared containing photographs and accounts by survivors. But when the May issue of *Sunset* was published, a cover by famed artist Maynard Dixon depicted a female figure representing "The Spirit of the City." Stressing "New San Francisco," the magazine offered three pages credited to Edward H. Harriman, president of Southern Pacific. He wrote of "wonderful conditions" in the city and of plans to rebuild it along modern, earthquake-proof and fire-resistant lines. He also heaped praise on Schmitz, Funston, the Navy, and the California National Guard.

On the back page of the May issue of *Sunset*, accompanied by a Dixon drawing, was a poem by Charles K. Field, who had written the ode that asked why God had let churches be wrecked but saved Hotaling's Whiskey. Titled "The Choice," the poem's subjects were the fire and building a better city:

"Choose!" cried the Fiend, and his breath
  Withered the blossoming city;
"I am Destruction and Death,–
  Choose! Is it greed now, or pity?
Ye have been given this hour,
  Hardly I wait on your pleasure,
What will you save from my power,
  Life or your treasure?"

Then with one voice they replied:
  "All that earth hath in its giving
Reckon we nothing beside
  Even the least of the living;
Light in a dog's eyes, the bird
  Caged for its song,–beyond measure
These at the last are preferred,
  Love over treasure!"

So, having chosen, they fled
  And the Fiend took their treasures forsaken.
Lo, how their spirit was fed
  By the burden of love they had taken!
All unbereaved they behold,
  Dreams of their faith realizing,
A city more fair than their old
  Already uprising.

But the portrait of the city provided to the War Department on April 26, 1906, by General Greely was far different. Headed "Confidential," it reported, "Assumed control of distribution and supplies today. Officers and inspectors report fearful conditions indicating demoralization, dishonesty, and deception as might reasonably be expected from irregular services, voluntary and in many cases unorganized, this despite every effort on the part [of a] few devoted men who have worn themselves out in a task well nigh impossible."

Although conditions were "appalling," the general gamely averred he was not ready to "acknowledge incapacity to bring order and efficiency out of existing chaos."

Eighteen

※

BETTER THAN THE COUNTY JAIL

※

*W*HEN GENERAL GREELY SENT HIS FIRST report to Washington, he noted that in the week after the earthquake the Army issued a million rations to feed two hundred and fifty thousand people, more than half the city's population.

In reporting this statistic, the San Francisco *Chronicle* also noted, "To the hobos and tramps that infest San Francisco in large numbers throughout the year, the earthquake came as a forerunner of a time of plenty. Amid the general destitution which the country at large is doing its utmost to relieve, the tramps are passing themselves off as sufferers of the disaster, and in consequence, they are living much better than they usually fare. They do not even have to beg for food; it is given to them cheerfully, for rather than let one needy person suffer, the committee in charge of the relief work is willing to take chances of feeding a hundred of the unworthy."

A case in point was "one of the more notorious members of the fraternity" of drifters on the waterfront. Known as "Shifty Bill," he "expressed himself to the effect that it was better than spending the winter in the County Jail."

Another staggering figure of the week after the quake was cited in a *Chronicle* headline:

VAST ARMY HAS LEFT THE CITY
SOUTHERN PACIFIC ALONE HAS TAKEN AWAY
OVER 225,000 REFUGEES

Between six o'clock in the morning on Wednesday, April 18, and Sunday night, April 22, the railroad had used more than nine hundred cars in 129 trains to take refugees on its main line from the Oakland depot to eastern points. During the same period, 610 suburban trains departed the Oakland pier. Because all these passengers were carried without charge, the Southern Pacific estimated its loss at $400,000. While this effort was made with a humanitarian motive, it had an element of smart public relations that muted widespread criticism, led by President Roosevelt, of railways as greedy giants that could be restrained only by actions of the federal government.

This feeling of goodwill to railroads persisted for many months in the minds of quake victims. Historian Charles Eugene Banks said in his book *The History of the San Francisco Disaster*, "The big railroads were no longer 'soulless corporations.' Instead, they were not only winged messengers of mercy, but they were messengers of colossal strength and bore in their giant arms thousands of tons of food and clothing for the starving and naked. They did this without money and without price. From New York to San Francisco; from the north to south; trains could be seen speeding along, bearing the grateful banner, 'Relief Train for the San Francisco Sufferers.' All freight and passenger traffic had to give the right-of-way to these relief trains, which ran at top speed and halted only for necessary coaling and water to keep the engines going. The express [freight] companies were no less liberal and carried everything offered that could in any way alleviate the sufferings, or strengthen the hopes of the destitute, huddled in the parks of San Francisco."

In a message to Roosevelt on April 26, Victor Metcalf reported "extraordinary efforts on the part of the water company" to meet the demand, "although it cannot be delivered in sufficient quantities for proper sanitation and fire purposes for some time." Four "trained mounted officers" were assigned to sanitation-inspection patrols of the entire city. As a result, Metcalf assured the White House, "The health of the city is remarkably good, everything considered."

Until the Army delivered rations, food supplies were an acute problem. "Little remained in San Francisco except in the area swept by the fire, and the available supply could not last more than a few days," wrote historian Charles Morris. "Fresh meat disappeared early on Wednesday and only canned food and breadstuffs were left. All the foodstuffs coming in on [railway] cars were at once seized by order of the mayor and added to the scanty supply, the names of the consignees being taken that this material might eventually be paid for." Despite these efforts, the food shortage resulted in numerous instances of price gouging.

Looting was also a serious problem, and not only among civilians. Some members of the state militia, under orders to protect property, became pillagers on a grand scale. On April 28, Major and Judge Advocate William P. Humphreys, Second Provisional Brigade of the National Guard of California, reported after an investigation in the Portsmouth Square area that within the last three days between fifteen and twenty members of the First Provisional Brigade of militia had been arrested by sentries for looting the burned district. He forwarded a recommendation to headquarters that members of that brigade "be denied permission to cross the bay to San Francisco, and that, if possible, persons going to the eastern side of the bay on the ferry boats having with them articles which are clearly loot should have these taken away from them," and that any guardsmen caught looting "be placed in the guard house."

Stepping into this maelstrom on Tuesday, April 24, was Dr. Edward Devine of the Red Cross. Designated by President Roosevelt to handle the relief effort, he was also expected to satisfy Roosevelt's concerns about civic corruption by ensuring that Mayor Schmitz and officials of his administration had as little as possible to do with the control of money and supplies. The relief committee faced its first task the following day, with the arrival of William Randolph Hearst's relief train. A military train also came with one hundred men and officers who'd crossed the country in three sleeper cars. Due that night from Chicago was a "medical special." Arranged by the Red Cross Society and the White Cross Society, it carried seventy-five nurses and doctors.

When trains also brought a growing number of sightseers and the morbidly curious, the Berkeley *Reporter* protested and warned in headlines:

WHEN YOU GO TO SAN FRANCISCO SEEK TO
RELIEVE SUFFERING
Stricken City is No Place for Idle Curious and Shallow People
Who Make a Mockery of Misery Caused by Fire and Quake

The article read:

Here's a suggestion for a sign that would look well on the seaward front of the shattered Ferry Building–painted in red letters ten feet long, and the whole front, so that he who runs may read. Also that he who reads may run:

"Do you come bearing gifts, and to relieve distress? Come in and WELCOME.

Or do you come to see the signs, and to prowl among the ashes for plunder? Then STAY OUT! THIS MEANS YOU!"

The trans-ferry boats are crowded and most of the passengers are those who go to gratify curiosity. Among them are those who go for the first time to look upon the desolation of their homes, and to search the ruins for whatever of value may be left, or perchance to look for some precious keepsake of those who lost their lives in the roaring hell of flame. And many of these find a crowd of ghouls pawing over the ashes, keeping what they find, and cackling with glee over possession of trinkets filched from the wreckage. While the stricken ones stand sadly by, dumb with sorrow and dry-eyed because the spring of tears is spent, the empty hee-haw of vacant minds rings echoing among bare, ghostly walls, as the incongruities of chaos appeal to the small sense of humor possessed by rudimentary brains.

A special correspondent of the *Chicago Record-Herald* reported on Monday, April 23, "The committee on feeding the hungry reports the most satisfactory progress in the huge task before it, and has already established fifty-two stations where all the hungry may secure their daily rations. Besides the government and the general food committees, which are doing the most heroic work, a large number of independent organizations are attacking the food problem." Lines of applicants at food stations stretched for blocks, but everyone received rations for one person as many times a day as requested. Reaching a food station was made easier by a limited restoration of the street railway system. Communication within the city and the outside world by telegraph and telephone was gradually being restored by the Signal Corps, connecting the Army's headquarters and Mayor Schmitz's office at Fort Mason with the Hall of Justice, the U.S. Mint, and the link to Oakland at the Ferry Building.

City Engineer Thomas P. Woodward sent a report that three investigative parties were sent out to ascertain whether or not the city as a whole had sunk. They found the "most notable depression" confined almost entirely to lower parts of the city, and "particularly to made ground."

Never in the history of the United States had so many citizens been left homeless and hungry. Nearly three times as many were dispossessed by the earthquake and fire than in the Great Chicago Fire of 1871. Long-since rebuilt, proud of its new reputation for architectural grandeur, and claiming the title of America's "second city" in wealth and culture, Chicago chose to express sympathy with San Francisco, and provide tangible assistance in the form of money, by acting on a suggestion from the chairman of its relief committee and publisher of the *Chicago Examiner.* Andrew M. Lawrence proposed that the city sponsor "the most stupendous theatrical benefit performance ever known."

Nineteen

❧

FOR THE BENEFIT OF
SAN FRANCISCO

❧

*W*HEN AMERICA'S LEADING ENTERTAINERS put on fund-raising shows within hours after the destruction of the World Trade Center on September 11, 2001, they probably did not realize that they were emulating the most celebrated entertainers in the early years of the 20th century. Shows "for the benefit of San Francisco" were held from coast to coast.

Madame Sarah Bernhardt, the era's most revered actress, was deeply moved by the San Francisco tragedy and immediately responded to the idea of a theatrical benefit in a Chicago lakefront park. She promised not only to take part, but also to lend the city a giant tent that had been made to accommodate huge audiences for her recent show in Texas. She also offered that her manager, W. F. Connor, be general director of the benefit.

One of the nation's foremost theatrical managers, George W. Lederer, signed on to serve as stage manager. A. Jacobs of Chicago's Olympic Theater joined the effort as house manager. Also from the Olympic, C. E. Kohl would be the show's director. The Garrick Theater's manager, Sam P. Gerson, was chosen as treasurer of the fund with responsibility for the tickets. Publicity was put into the hands of George S. Wood of the Colonial Theater.

With Bernhardt's participation declared and Thursday, April 26, announced as the date of the show, the Chicago Federation of Musicians, perhaps mindful that San Francisco's mayor was a violinist and had been president of the city's musicians' union, offered five hundred of its members to provide accompaniments to performers. Contributing to the effort was Local No. 2 of the Theatrical Stage Employees International Alliance, providing the services of electricians, stagehands, and carpenters at no charge. The John Gillespie Lumber Company provided all necessary lumber for the event. The "Bernhardt Tent," as it became known, was transported by the Chicago & Alton Railroad, which also brought Madame Bernhardt from Indianapolis, Indiana, and would later convey her to Peoria, Illinois—the next stop on her national tour. With lighting at no cost from the Chicago Edison Company, erection of the tent and other smaller shelters would be done by the United States Tent and Awning Company, assisted by a team of canvas raisers from the Ringling Brothers Circus. Raised on the Lake Front Park opposite the Auditorium Hotel, the massive tent had room for 6,500 seats.

Festivities commenced at 10:30 Thursday morning with a concert by the 500-piece band that lasted till noon. "What a glorious picture it was," wrote Charles Eugene Banks. "Buildings, viaduct, boulevard and park a mass of humanity, quiet and sympathic. There was not an ill-natured person among all those thousands. It was more like a religious service than an amusement. One great family gathered to assist and comfort and soothe a wounded member of the household could not have been more universal in their feelings and deportment."

As a tribute to Madame Berndhardt's native country, the band played the French national anthem, timed to coincide with the pressing of a button by President Theodore Roosevelt in the White House, sending an electrical charge that rang a gong that signaled a booming salute by a cannon and the simultaneous raising and unfurling of the

French and American flags. This was followed by Mr. Lederer reading "greetings" from Roosevelt with "best wishes for the success of the benefit performance for the relief of the San Francisco sufferers."

Taking the stage after a prolonged ovation, Bernhardt recited a poem by Victor Hugo, then said in French, "The calamity which has struck San Francisco has had an echo in the hearts of the people of the entire world. But those who, like myself, have had the joy of visiting that admirable city have the feeling of a yet deeper sorrow. Nevertheless, as evil brings with itself some good, I, who know the great American nation, think that like the phoenix, San Francisco will rise again from the ashes greater, more beautiful and stronger against the furore of the elements. The public of Chicago, to whom I owe so much happiness and to whom I am so much indebted, has once more provided its kindness to me by coming under my tent to bring its share of offerings, thus allowing me to take a very small part in that brotherly impulse of the United States toward her unfortunate sister."

Popular singers Florence Holbrook and Cecil Lean with the La Salle Theater Chorus kicked off the afternoon's entertainment program. Robert Hunter's Company from Chicago's Grand Opera House performed an act from *Before and After*. Elizabeth Will sang "Chicago Says I Will." Carle and Adele Rowland offered a selection from a current hit musical, *The Mayor of Tokio*. Performances then followed with more songs by Mr. and Mrs. H. L. Waterhouse; actors in *Mrs. Wiggs and the Cabbage Patch* (then playing at McCicker's Theater); Buster Brown and his dog, Tige (starring at the Great Northern Theater); E. E. Sothern and Julia Marlowe with act two of *The Taming of the Shrew* (then at the Illinois Theater).

Others on the long program were Trixie Friganza from the Chicago Opera House; E. S. Willard from the Colonial reciting "The Charge of the Light Brigade"; La Petite Adelaide, "the little dancer" of the "Three Graces Company"; artist T. A. O'Shaughnessy with some "rapid sketches"; Robert Loraine and his company and automobile from Power's Theater in an act from *Man and Superman*; one act of Studebaker Theater's *The College Widow*; and Louis Harrison and Miss Caro Roma with songs from the Garrick Theater production of *Mexicana.*

Among tunes played by the musicians' union band in pauses between performers and during intermissions was Eugene Schmitz's march, "The Yankee Hustler," composed before Abraham Ruef talked him into running for mayor of San Francisco.

Total receipts from the benefit: $15,605. Money was also raised through brisk sales of souvenirs. A box of cigars went for $61; four boxes of Cracker Jack for $18. A tablecover with autographs of all the performers brought $105. George Lederer exclaimed, "I have been in benefits held in London, Paris and New York, but never have I witnessed one on a parity with that held on the Lake Front. Never before in my theatrical career have I seen so successful an entertainment."

But Chicago wasn't finished. An annual actors' benefit that had previously been planned for Friday, April 27, directed the proceeds to San Francisco relief. Mayor Dunne declared that Saturday would be "San Francisco Day" and that every policeman would go from house to house on his beat collecting contributions so that no one "willing to contribute should be overlooked." Ranging from a quarter to five dollars, donations gathered by police amounted to nearly $35,000. A concert on Sunday with a talk by orchestra leader Dwight Elmendorf on the subject of San Francisco realized $1,289 for the relief fund. A few days later, the Apollo Music Club and the Thomas Orchestra raised money at a performance of Haydn's "The Creation."

New York's benefit on Sunday, April 29, was held in the city's biggest showplace, the Hippodrome. Leading a 350-piece orchestra was the country's most beloved composer of popular music, Victor Herbert. His show, *Babes in Toyland,* had been running at San Francisco's Columbia Theater, a showplace that was now a ruin. Names on the program that would mean nothing to Americans a century later, unless they are students of the theater, but were among the greatest musical stars in 1906, included Madame Schumann-Heink, Eugene Cowles, and Miss Blanche Duffield. They joined a grand chorus of five hundred from the Fritzi Scheff Opera Company and a dozen vaudeville artists, along with the Free Lance Opera from the Hippodrome Company, before a capacity audience of New York's café and high society.

"While Chicago and New York gave the biggest benefits," noted Charles Eugene Banks, "others were given in nearly every city, town and village in all the broad land. There were baseball games, athletic contests, billiard tournaments, concerts, lectures and amateur entertainments without number. And the receipts from all of them went to swell the mighty flood of gold that poured steadily westward to the ruined city of the Golden Gate."

Twenty

❀

PLANS ARE AFOOT

❀

"ONFIDENCE IN SAN FRANCISCO IS UNSHAKEN," reported Richard Fairchild to the *Chicago Record-Herald* on April 26. "With the ruins of its great retail and wholesale buildings still smoking, plans are afoot for their reconstruction. San Francisco rebuilt is to be a better, a safer and a more comfortable city for business and residential purposes that it was before. Capital in abundance to work the miracle is at hand. Chicago and New York financiers are ready with it. The Harrimans, the Stillmans, the Rockefellers and Morgans of the financial world are anxious to expedite the work." Instead of dooming San Francisco, he continued, "the double attack of fire and quake will prove a blessing."

A blueprint for a new San Francisco was already on file. Leading San Franciscans calling themselves the Association for the Improvement and Adornment of San Francisco had commissioned it in 1904. Prepared by distinguished Chicago architect Daniel H. Burnham, and approved in September of 1905 by Mayor Schmitz, it was inspired by the boulevard system of Paris. Burnham envisioned a great, broad, dignified, encircling waterfront drive. Within it would be smaller concentric rings separated by wide avenues that enclosed a grand civic center. In it would be City Hall, the Court of Justice,

Customs House, Appraisers' Building, State Building, Post Office, and other government structures. From the center would radiate diagonal arteries like spokes of a wheel, but shaped to conform to the topography of the city's famous hills.

The "Burnham Plan" called for public and private structures "of monumental character and of great civic interest," including a library, opera house, concert hall, municipal theater, museum of natural history, academy of art, academy of music, and exhibition and assembly halls. On the chief radial avenue, in recognition of the significance of railroads in the city's history and to its economy, would rise the Union Railway Station, "forming a vestibule to the heart of the city." Recognizing that San Francisco was born of the meeting of sea captains and gold seekers, and was, as Mayor Schmitz reminded the President of the United States, the country's golden gate to the Pacific, the design provided for "indefinite expansion" of docks and warehouses. Another feature of the plan was a system of underground transit, a dream that would not be realized for more than half a century in the form of BART, the Bay Area Rapid Transit.

Even as General Funston's soldiers, Lieutenant Freeman's sailors, and city fire fighters were struggling to stop the conflagration, real estate men, builders, architects, and city officials were meeting in Oakland, eager to begin the profitable work of rebuilding. Prominent among them were representatives of iron- and steel-producing companies with reminders that buildings with steel-cage construction had weathered the earthquake.

"The tall structures fashioned in the modern way withstood the shock best," Richard Fairfield informed readers of his Chicago newspaper. In a concise analysis of the reason so much damage had resulted from the quake, he continued, "Buildings with brick walls tied to a steel frame seemed invulnerable. The local theory of building, by the same token, was demonstrated deficient. Walls that were not securely attached to their frames fell out or crumbled into heaps. The Claus Spreckles Building, in which the San Francisco *Call* was published, is intact. It was built after the plan of the First National Bank

Building in Chicago or the Flatiron Building in New York. Its neighbors, constructed by the San Francisco method, are on the ground. Many foundations were too light. Some were nothing more than piles driven into the ground. In the new San Francisco considerable attention is to be paid to sub-construction work."

Repairs and reconstruction costs also came under prompt consideration in Washington, D.C. Forwarded to the Secretary of the Treasury on April 29 by Secretary of War William Howard Taft were "urgent deficiency estimates of appropriations" amounting to $3,387,630. The money was for the fiscal year ending on June 30 and requested to cover the costs of replacing military stores destroyed by the earthquake, fixing telegraph cables between the city and Alcatraz and Angel islands, and damage to the Presidio Hospital. Funds would also be required to repair the post offices.

Before most of this work could commence, electric and gas lines had to be restored. The responsibility rested with the San Francisco Gas and Electric Company. While finding that most of the plants and sub-stations would be "out of commission for some time," the company vowed quick resumption of the Protrero operation, allowing rapid connection of street arc lights on three routes encompassing the unburned district and various industrial plants. A second electric firm, Mutual Electric Light and Power, announced that its Spear Street plant only suffered damage to a water line and that the facility would be at full power within a few days. The provision of gas and water would take much longer because all underground mains had been ruptured.

The devastation of 490 city blocks and nearly thirty thousand buildings, with an estimated value of between $350 million and $500 million, represented about two-thirds of the city's property tax base and roughly a third of the state's taxable real estate.

In addition to the commercial cost was the toll taken on the city's institutions of culture and art, from the Grand Opera House and the Hopkins Institute of Art to the Memorial Museum in Golden Gate Park. On April 28, a reporter for the *Chronicle* found the Egyptian-style, stucco front of the building shattered and the interior "a sad wreck." The newspaper account noted, "The china room would make a collector or a careful housewife weep. Many of the beautiful vases are ruined, and all the statuary was thrown down and broken. The show cases were generally smashed and the work of cleaning up and estimating the damage, now going on, is considerable."

The reporter added a macabre touch. "Some of the mummies, after surviving the trials and vicissitudes of some 5,000 or 6,000 years," he wrote, "were smashed to bits."

The earthquake had also disturbed the repose of the more recently deceased. "In all of the cemeteries this side of the county line the effect of the shock is to be seen," reported the *Chronicle* on May 6. "Were one to carefully examine all the monuments in Calvary, Masonic, Laurel Hill, Odd Fellows' and the old city cemetery the result would be astonishing. The keeper of one of these cemeteries ventured it as his opinion that there weren't three pieces of stone in his cemetery that hadn't been disturbed in some way or another."

At a time when "the clatter of the hammer and the buzz saw are heard throughout the burned section of San Francisco, and temporary bungalows are sprouting on the ground where once stood more substantial and handsomer structures," wrote the *Chronicle* reporter, "out in the silent acres of the dead nothing has been done as yet toward repairing the damage wrought by the big earthquake."

He found that the quake had struck gravesites in peculiar ways, but the most curious of all "the freaks in and around the grave yards" was found in a little stoneyard opposite the entrance to the Masonic Cemetery. Two small monuments standing about four feet high and each built of three solid blocks of marble and identical in everything except color had been affected identically by the quake. "The top of one section of each monument now stands exactly in the place it was put by the cutter. The midsection of each, however, has moved in a straight line a little over a fraction of three inches eastward. In other words, the top of each monument has not been disturbed, while the large block between the top and base has moved more than three inches out of alignment. How this could have happened seems inconceivable. It resembles the trick performed by certain dexterous jugglers who pull a tablecloth from a table without disturbing the position of the dishes."

The "temporary bungalows" mentioned in the newspaper article were eight thousand in number. These barracks-style dwellings accommodated six to eight families. For many occupants, the structures were better than the homes from which they'd fled, and for all refugees they were certainly an improvement over the "tent cities" that had sprouted in city parks. Men who'd been thrown out of work because their places of employment had collapsed or gone up in flames left these makeshift havens from the elements to take jobs in the reconstruction of a city that began even while the fires were raging.

"The way in which shattered, scorched San Francisco shook off the ashes and debris and set about the mighty task of building a new city, greater and grander than the old," Charles Eugene Banks wrote, "was a most inspiring example of American pluck and courage."

One of the heaviest losers of property, William Crocker, nephew of Central Pacific co-founder William H. Crocker, said, "Mark my words, San Francisco will arise from these ashes a greater and more beautiful city than ever. I don't take any stock in the belief of some people that investors and residents will be panicky and afraid to build up again. This calamity, terrible as it is, will mean nothing less than a new and grander San Francisco. It is preposterous to suggest abandonment of the city. It is the natural metropolis of the Pacific Coast. God made it so."

The challenge was formidable. Government buildings and most archives were gone. The only bank to escape destruction or serious damage was the Market Street National. Twenty-nine schools had been flattened and 44 damaged. Hospitals and churches were in ruins. Most foundries and factories on the waterfront were wrecked. The only remnants of homes were the brick chimneys that poked out of the rubble in all directions. Nob Hill palaces resembled the ruins of ancient Rome. Great hotels were burned-out hulks. Theaters and opera houses were reduced to ash. Streets were open wounds bleeding precious water.

Yet, here and there, on walls that were all that remained of once-thriving businesses or houses, people who had lost everything but a sense of humor had scrawled defiance and resolution in the oldest form of written communication. Among the graffiti was found:

> The cow is in the hammock
> The cat is in the lake,
> The baby in the garbage can,
> What difference does it make?
> There is no water, and still less soap.
> We have no city, but lots of hope.

Another wag inscribed:

> First to shake
> First to burn
> First to take
> Another new turn.

On green shutters of a makeshift kitchen in a refugee camp, someone in despair wrote:

> Out in the world,
> Out in the street.

Below this, an optimist answered the plaint with a rhyme:

> But what's the use of kicking
> When you've got enough to eat?

Perhaps the most illuminating piece of graffiti, portraying San Francisco's spirit, advised, "Eat, drink and be merry, for tomorrow we may have to go to Oakland."

Twenty-One

❀

RASCALITY IN EVERY STREET

❀

"FROM SUCH GREAT DISASTERS MAN DISCOVERS his own helplessness," wrote Charles Eugene Banks and co-author Opie Read in the preface to their book on the quake. "It is the recognition of this truth that moves men to lean upon one another; to accept kindness without question and to in turn be helpful."

Beginning with the first shocking news flashes from the only surviving telegraph station in Oakland, the outpouring of material and financial aid across the nation was great and swift. A request by President Roosevelt that Congress appropriate half a million dollars was granted within ten minutes. General Funston's plea to the War Department that tents and other supplies be sent was responded to immediately. Relief trains organized by William Randolph Hearst and others began rolling westward, followed by funds collected by theatrical benefits and offering plates passed around in countless churches.

So much food, clothing, and temporary shelter had been provided by the end of April that the *Chronicle* declared, "Thousands of our people have been living far better than they ever lived in their lives." But the newspaper also noted "unwise expenditure of relief funds by local committees." A week later, the newspaper's editorial found "rascality in every street" and noted that "a good deal of swindling has been done by contractors, by putting in foundations for buildings in this city in which mud was made to masquerade for cement."

Irate over the "crowning sorrow" of the relief distribution, physician Margaret Mahoney complained that only "a small part has reached the refugees, for whom the relief was sent." It was "red tape and system," she said, that prevented "those who lost their all from receiving proper care."

In large measure because President Roosevelt had sound reasons for distrusting Mayor Schmitz's honesty, the distribution of relief money was placed, by presidential decree, into the hands of Dr. Edward Devine of the Red Cross Society. He worked with a finance committee headed by former mayor James D. Phelan, a leading critic of Schmitz's administration. Though Phelan and Dr. Devine had stellar ethical reputations, it was not sufficient to dispel a public belief expressed by Dr. Mahoney that blame for faults in the relief system must be placed upon "the combination of Red Cross, trained charity workers, and a relief committee composed of wealthy men." With six million dollars in relief money floating around, suspicions grew that a large chunk of the funds was finding its way into the pockets of entrenched grafters.

Doubters discerned evidence of shady doings in 80,000 barrels of flour that had been sent from the Midwest via Minneapolis. Because it was of no use to refugees who did their cooking on open fires or with primitive stoves without ovens for baking, the Relief Committee chose to auction it to commercial bakeries. When word spread that 100-pound sacks of flour were being stored in a warehouse, a mob of women from Jefferson Park Refugee Camp stormed the doors. Dismayed and disgusted by the riot, and worried that the U.S. Army would be criticized, General Greely shot off a letter to Secretary of War Taft:

> So far the entire relief system has been administered by the Army and so far no scandals or frictions have developed.

Unfortunately, a scandal is in the air connected with the selling of about seven thousand tons of flour by the Red Cross Finance Committee, but in this matter the Army has had absolutely nothing to do as I carefully refrained from giving any assistance in any way, stating that it was a commercial transaction which must be handled by the Finance Committee.

While Greely attributed the flour sale to "a case of bad judgment," the common feeling among the refugees was that graft had raised its ugly head.

Further fomenting this distrust were a group of socialists calling themselves the "Tammany Civic Association." They charged that relief funds had been "looted and stolen and the poor refugees humiliated, starved, and reduced to hapless conditions by the conduct of their self-constituted guardians." They also contended that Rudolph Spreckles of the Relief Committee was "captain general of a horde of petty tyrants and camp commanders" who subjected refugees to indignities, denials, and deprivations, "which a people less forbearing would meet with arms and a heroic determination to take the lives of the thieves and overlords and petty tyrants that were degrading them."

General Greely, increasingly eager to pull the Army from the city and leave the relief efforts in the hands of civilian authority, wired Taft in early May: "Continued exercise of police power by troops and enforcement of military sanitary regulations on public parks and other city grounds must inevitably lead to a clash of authority and consequent discredit to the Army. During past fortnight have been frequently advised that political complications were developing and questions of public responsibility would be dodged by securing retention of Army and developing decisions on matters affecting municipality and state or federal authorities through the Army." When Mayor Schmitz and the Relief Committee petitioned Taft to keep the Army in the city, their plea prevailed. U.S. troops would remain in San Francisco until July 1, 1906.

In the interim, Schmitz and the Relief Committee regarded the troops as the chief means of maintaining law and order in the relief camps and among their increasingly restless, irritable, and suspicious residents. This decision was favored by one of Boston's prominent newspapers, the *Traveler*. Its June 27, 1906, issue noted, "The army went about the work of policing the city and bringing about sanitation and good order in a business-like way, and it is due all praise for the results accomplished. Without the army there would probably [have] been anarchy and chaos."

But the paper also sounded an alarm. An article, "The San Francisco Situation," reported, "The saddest news that comes from the West is that Mayor Schmitz of San Francisco who in the period immediately following the catastrophe, surprised his friends and delighted them by his energy, ability and broadness, is slipping back into the clutches of Abe Ruef, the boss of San Francisco, who has run things in that city practically as he pleased for years."

Theodore Roosevelt's handpicked relief director was also faulted. "The work of Dr. Devine," said the *Traveler*, "has not been satisfactory." Declaring "characteristic red tape" not acceptable to a people "who are not asking for charity, but relief," and expressing concern over plans for "organizing an independent committee that will be responsible for these funds," the newspaper opined, "To turn money raised in various states for the purpose of relief over to any board of aldermen or supervisors controlled by Abe Ruef, is out of the question; and so far as the Massachusetts relief committee is concerned, it will not be done."

While Abraham Ruef had remained aloof from the activities of Mayor Schmitz's fifty-man emergency committee, he was a highly visible figure on city streets as they went up in flames. One of his first acts was to arrange the evacuation of his parents to a German steamer, the *Uarad*, where they remained for the duration of the fire. He had supplied dynamite in the effort to save his Commercial Hotel. As the fire threatened the North Beach area, he'd grabbed a hose from one of the fire department wagons until Lieutenant

Frederick Freeman drew a pistol and held him at gunpoint while firemen took it back.

Having welcomed the destruction of Chinatown as an opportunity to turn the area into a lucrative business development, Ruef noted that the majority of Chinese had fled to refugee camps in Oakland. With fewer than two hundred in a camp set aside for them (Camp No. 3 above Fort Point in the Presidio), he formed an alliance with James Phelan in a committee appointed by Schmitz to find a new location for Chinatown, but, as noted earlier, the plan did not materialize.

Success came easier in matters of restoring trolley car and telephone service. Through "fees" that, in part, went to bribe city supervisors, Ruef ignored public opinion and gained approval for United Railroads to save the cost of repairing underground wires by stringing power cables overhead. For another fee, a monopoly phone franchise was awarded without opposition to the Home Telephone Company.

Both these achievements would soon come back to plague him, as would his attempt to reestablish a lucrative pre-quake enterprise—a collaboration with Mayor Schmitz in granting and renewing liquor licenses for "French restaurants." Providing elegant dining on the ground floor for men and their families or business clients, they offered more intimate surroundings on the second floor for men entertaining women who were not their wives. The upper floors provided amenities for which food was unimportant.

Without a liquor license, these establishments could not exist. Eager to restore income from them as soon as possible, Ruef encountered no difficulty in persuading his partner, Mayor Schmitz, to rescind the ban on liquor sales and to allow saloons to resume business. Hearing of this, General Greely became even more determined to withdraw the Army. He felt that any city that allowed the sale of liquor was capable of handling resulting policing problems by itself.

With July 5 announced as the date for restoration of liquor sales, coincidentally with the departure of the Army, the growing chorus of criticism of city government on the issue of relief was joined by voices of a national "temperance movement." Attackers of "Demon Rum" had long pointed to the city by the bay as a prime example of the evils of intoxicating drinks, not only regarding their ruinous effect on individuals and the American family, but as a major cause of corruption of government officials through political bosses and masterminds of the payoff, of whom Abraham Ruef and Mayor Eugene Schmitz were cited as deplorable examples.

Charles Moore in the August 6, 1906, issue of *California Voice*, expressed typical prohibitionist outrage. Noting that he had visited San Francisco many times in the previous three months to arrange free distribution of milk among the refugees, and that he'd been interested in the temperance cause for many years, he wrote, "I observed the different moves made by the saloons and saw to my disgust how anxious they were to work again on the same old grab."

He continued:

> I wish that every citizen would remember that San Francisco, during the absence of the saloon, was the cleanest and most moral city in the entire world. This should be a lesson forever of what a grand place this world would be to live in when the saloon shall cease to exist, and I firmly believe that some time that day will come.
>
> Temperance people throughout our entire land should [give] honor where honor is due, to Generals Funston and Greely for keeping the saloon closed so long. But you can imagine my disgust when the famous San Francisco brand of grafters decided that the saloons were to reopen on July 5th, and now things are getting worse every week.
>
> One of the most conspicuous signs displayed on the streets is "Anheuser-Busch on draught 5 cts."
>
> All of which reminds me that some brewer in St. Louis put a hundred thousand dollars into the Relief Fund, which was accompanied by many newspaper writeups and much hot air

about the generosity of the giver. But I don't understand any form of generosity which would teach that one human being should take from other human beings millions of dollars through such an infamous business as the open saloon, and give back to those people this hundred thousand dollars which would be one percent of the brewery which has been wrung from the earnings of the laboring class during the past twenty or thirty years.

Prohibitionists such as Moore, who did not find it surprising to learn that heroic efforts had been made to save the Hotaling Whiskey warehouse, could only observe despairingly while saloons opened to brisk business. But, in fact, the dispensing of strong drink had never ceased. While surviving saloons and liquor stores had been closed by Funston's soldiers and city police, a thousand improvised bars had been set up amid the ruins, including the appropriately named The Phoenix in a South of Market boardinghouse.

Eager to get back in stride, Jerome Bassity lost no time in letting it be known that he planned to build the world's largest whorehouse. This did not mean that the quake and fire had put an end to prostitution. While the brothels of San Francisco had been flattened by the quake or burned out, opportunities for carnality abounded across the bay. Oakland Police Chief Walter J. Peterson recalled to the *Bulletin,* "San Francisco was still smoldering, the earth still rocking, and we didn't know when the Almighty might send another visitation, yet on the incessant demand [of men], the authorities [of Oakland] had to open up the houses of prostitution. All day long and at night men were lined up for blocks waiting in front of the houses, like a box office at a theater on a popular night."

In San Francisco, a woman known as Madame Labrodet opened a house at Turk and Steiner Streets, which operated successfully for several months after the quake. Other resorts had brief tenures, while some enjoyed longer success. By 1910, there were nearly three hundred saloons and dance halls crowded into six blocks around Pacific Street—more than had existed on the main thorough-fare of the Barbary Coast prior to the earthquake. A result of the de-mand for such properties was skyrocketing rents. Basement and street-level space, which if rented to a legitimate business would not have brought more than thirty to a hundred dollars a month, earned the property owner ten times as much from vice merchants. A ten-year lease for a sixty-by-thirty-foot cellar went for nine hundred dol-lars a month.

Rents became a bone of contention when the Red Cross Relief Committee proposed that refugees pay for their housing in camps or be evicted. Leading the protest against such payments, the Tammany Civic Federation distributed a flyer exhorting "refugees and com-rades" to "pay no rent to the Red Cross." Over the name of Alva Udell, "Chairman of Provisional Committee," it said, "When these reprehensible creatures, or any one of them, in the presence of reli-able witnesses, threaten under color of official right, to evict you from your homes, unless you pay rent for cottages built in the parks, or on other public lands, with relief funds, then pay the rent under threats, and report the facts to me. It is the obtaining of the rents, or other money, from you, with your consent induced by wrongful use of force or fear, under color of official right, that constitutes the crime of extortion; and we want your assistance in bringing the criminals to account for their crimes."

Udell also petitioned President Roosevelt and Secretary of War Taft to remove relief funds from the custody of the Relief Committee. In a second printed circular, issued by "The Committee of Whole," Dr. Edward Devine, James Phelan, and relief committee member Allan Pollock, were branded "traitors" and told that if their resigna-tions weren't handed in at once they would be tarred and feathered.

Further inflammation of refugee anger toward the Red Cross was a "census" conducted in the camps of "unattached" women. They were defined as either respectable women with a desire to work, respectable women who would not work, "unfortunate" women who desired to "reform," or "unfortunate" women who were "hopeless." Evidently to keep them from turning to prostitution, those not willing to work were moved into special camps, "before the army retires and the saloons are again opened."

Countering the protests by the refugees were residents who lived adjacent to the Lafayette Square camps. Pointing to the Tammany Civic Association as proof that such settlements had become "hotbeds of socialism," they demanded that the camps be demolished and "troublemakers" be sent elsewhere. This triggered a mass meeting of refugees that was led by a woman who lived in Tent 1, Section C. Mrs. J. W. Scott struck a San Francisco *Call* reporter as "almost handsomely attired." On her earlobes "sparkled brilliant diamonds, at her throat was a valuable diamond sunburst, and rich gems sparkled on her white hands," as she seemingly betrayed her own social class.

"There is but one reason why the people of Lafayette Square should be singled out for removal," Scott said, "and that is the objection of certain people of wealth to their presence. Which ought to be the first consideration, the whims of the rich or the absolute requirements of the unfortunate? By right the poor refugees have just as much claim on the property of the city as the people in mansions. The money that is being used was subscribed by outsiders for the benefit of the deserving who were burned out and could not pay heavy rents. My advice to you all is to stick together until the insult and wrong to us have been rectified."

Although a growing number of San Franciscans found reasons to express anger against the manner in which relief was being handled, and suspected that those in charge were engaging in graft, the vast majority of victims of the earthquake and fire were busy rebuilding with a light-hearted spirit. In an article titled "San Francisco at Play," in the October edition of the Southern Pacific Railroad's deliberately upbeat *Sunset* magazine, a New Yorker who had been in the city during the quake and stayed to take charge of relief work for the California Century Clubs of New York City disputed "gloomy descriptions" of a "desolate waste of ruins." Colonel Edwin Emerson, a

Spanish-American War veteran, a friend of Theodore Roosevelt, a lecturer, and a well-known writer, found San Francisco "still the gayest city of the Western Hemisphere." He wrote, "In truth I think it would be easier to change the leopard's spots than to shake all the laughter and love of fun out of merry hearted San Francisco."

Despite all sale of liquor being banned, he continued, "the town was as gay as ever." On an auto tour of "observation" with friends, Emerson had encountered "the same gay merry-makers at the Casino, the new Tait's, new Techau tavern and other reviving resorts, listening to the same old strains of music, as if all the joys of life were as plentiful and easily to be had on all sides as before the disaster." Among former residences and elsewhere in unharmed districts of the city, restaurants opened with their old names. They blossomed, Emerson thought, "like the clusters of wild lilies and nasturtiums that here and there have sprung from the ruins of former gardens in San Francisco flecking the dismal ashes with gleams of color and fragrance."

Theaters also rose in the ruins, led by the Central Theater under the shelter of a circus tent. "The taste for playgoing has become such a rage," said a stage manager, "that you can put on any old play, even the oldest chestnuts, and still there is standing room only."

In this rebuilding of San Francisco, Emerson found "hurry and hopefulness, gaiety, silken petticoats and starched gowns, corduroys, tramping boots, sombreros, temporary wooden buildings, the flutter of many flags, rush of automobiles, clatter of lumber, banging of hammers, and the rumble of drays—the very sunlit air seems to breathe renaissance."

As the city revived, Mayor Schmitz hoped that his actions in dealing with the quake and fire would combine with the forward-looking post-quake mood to make his pre-quake problem of an investigation into City Hall corruption and the bossism of Abe Ruef go away. Had the earthquake not occurred on April 18, a public inquiry would have begun that very day. Instead, the mayor who was to have been investigated appointed men who were to have conducted the probe to the Committee of Fifty, including former mayor James Phelan, Rudolph Spreckles, and attorney Garrett McEnerney. Another reason for Schmitz to hope his troubles had been buried in the rubble of the earthquake lay in the destruction that had befallen the offices of a newspaper that had been the instigator and implacable motivator of the investigation.

In the early days of Schmitz's administration, Fremont Older of the *Bulletin* had unleashed a team of reporters to uncover evidence of graft and proof of corrupting control by Abraham Ruef. But it was not until 1905 that Older found a powerful ally in the U.S. President, who had launched his own war against the corrupting power of railroads in general, and the Southern Pacific in particular. With Theodore Roosevelt's approval, a special federal prosecutor was named. San Francisco-born Francis J. Heney had earned a reputation as a corruption-buster in Oregon. Joining Heney was William J. Burns. The founder of a private detective agency, he was also Director of the Secret Service. To assist with the financing of the investigation, Older had turned to Rudolph Spreckles and James Phelan to contribute to a $100,000 fund. To make matters worse for Schmitz, Older had enlisted District Attorney William H. Langdon, an incorruptible Schmitz appointee who became an opponent of the Southern Pacific machine.

If proof was needed that Abe Ruef had resumed control of the city, Fremont Older, the bruised but still upright citizenry, and the revolutionary zealots in the refugee camps found it in the trial of National Guard Captain Ernest Denicke, who was charged with the murder of a sailor who may or may not have been engaging in looting. Abraham Ruef appeared as Denicke's attorney. When Denicke was released on bail, a scream went up from the newspaper *Socialist Voice.*

Noting that the charge had been sworn by "reputable citizens," but that bail had been granted, the paper asked, "Why?" Its answer: "Well, Abe Ruef, a lawyer with no reputation and a politician with no character, asked for it, aye, demanded it. Who is Abe Ruef? Well, he is the man the big city capitalists allow to own the city government. He is the owner and manipulator of a certain puppet known as

Mayor Schmitz; he has become wealthy through Tammany Hall methods of city deals, special grafts, inside information, holdups, and other forms of high finance and public looting."

While Captain Denicke was acquitted on the murder charge, Ruef had little time to savor his court victory. Amid the noise and tumult of the commencement of rebuilding San Francisco, the quake-interrupted investigators of Ruef and his influence over the Schmitz administration soon unearthed the machinations that resulted in the awarding of repair work in the street transit system, a telephone monopoly grant, and a deal to allow the gas company to break a pledge to reduce rates. It set them higher. Ruef achieved this through a system of bribes and payoffs. These new discoveries, combined with evidence gathered concerning corruption before the earthquake, resulted in indictments of Ruef, Mayor Schmitz, the chief of police, United Railroads supervisors, and officials of the telephone company and the gas and electric company.

Observing the impending downfall of Mayor Schmitz, the man in charge of the relief efforts, Dr. Edward Devine, hurried to assure San Franciscans and the people of the nation who had contributed money, that there was no graft in dispensing relief. Conceding that mistakes had been made, and that all the "unfortunates" of San Francisco had not been treated alike, Devine declared, "I can say to you that none of the people suffered for the necessities of life. There was none who was not supplied with food, clothing, bedding and shelter, and all that was absolutely necessary."

Although Abraham Ruef attempted to flee the city, he was tracked down and arrested on March 9, 1907, at the Trocadero roadhouse by court-appointed detectives and then held at the St. Francis Hotel because the police force could not be trusted. Ignoring his lawyer's advice, Ruef pleaded guilty to extortion on May 16. Weeping before the judge, he made himself appear to be a victim of the system of government corruption that he said he had hoped to change. Having failed, he said, he'd given into temptation and embraced the foul system he'd originally wanted to destroy.

Surprisingly, Ruef's act of contrition affected the man who had spent years going after him. Fremont Older of the *Bulletin* said, "I have tried to repent for the bitterness of spirit, the ignorance I displayed in pursuing the man Ruef, instead of attacking the wrong standard of society and a system which makes Ruefs inevitable. I may not have succeeded, but at least I have reached the point where I can see the good in the so-called bad people, and can forgive and plead that mercy be shown to Abraham Ruef."

Believing that Ruef could not have succeeded in corrupting government if he had not been able to manipulate the city's class animosities, Older faulted the people of San Francisco. If Ruef had not committed his "chief crime" of being "found out," he continued, "I feel sure that if he had escaped detection, even though we were possessed of a general knowledge of all that he had done, he would still be honored and respected in this community. So Ruef, after all, was punished for his failure, not for what he did."

Sentenced to prison at San Quentin, Ruef served seven years and returned to pursue real estate ventures in a recovering city that was well on its way to reclaiming its reputation as the jewel of the West Coast. Yet, amid all the wealth of the Golden Gate to the Pacific, he died in 1936 a bankrupt.

After a short period of deliberation, a jury convicted Mayor Schmitz of 27 counts of graft and bribery on June 14, 1907. The judge asserted that by being found guilty, he would "lose the respect and esteem of all good men." Evidently feeling that was punishment enough, the judge suspended a five-year sentence. When the conviction was reversed on appeal, San Franciscans proved generous to their good-natured mayor who had demonstrated leadership and heroism during its greatest crisis. Although they chose not to elect him mayor when he ran for the office in 1915 and 1919, they granted him a seat on the Board of Supervisors, which he held until 1925. When he died on November 20, 1928, several mayors and other officials served as pallbearers and men of the fire and police departments formed an honor guard.

A month after Schmitz's conviction, the Board of Supervisors chose one of their own to serve as mayor. Within days, Dr. Charles Boxton admitted having taken a bribe of $5,000 from the Home Telegraph Company and others. Resigning the mayoralty, he told a grand jury, "I never sought the honor."

Interviewed by the *Boston Herald* two days after Schmitz's conviction, James Phelan said that "the rout" of Ruef and Schmitz "at last brought the government of graft, which existed for several years in San Francisco, to an end." He went on to say that the city "is recovering from its great disaster with surprising and satisfactory speed," and that "in five years San Francisco will be a better city than ever before."

Eplilogue

✿

EAST IS EAST AND WEST IS SAN FRANCISCO

✿

*I*N 1909, SHORT-STORY AUTHOR AND extoller of the virtues of life in the city of New York, William Sydney Porter, better known as O. Henry, wrote that, according to Californians, "East is East and West is San Francisco."

In the same year in the city by the bay, in a bordello on O'Farrell Street, Tessie Wall, known to her clientele of mostly college boys as Miss Tessie, opened negotiations for possible sale of the house to big-time gambler Frank Daroux. Described by Herbert Asbury in *The Barbary Coast* as a flamboyant and well-upholstered blonde, she so impressed Frank when she drank 22 bottles of wine without having to excuse herself to use a toilet that Frank decided she was the gal for him. One hundred guests at their historic wedding feast consumed eighty cases of champagne (960 bottles, or about 240 gallons). When Frank said that he didn't want to compete in the same business as his bride, he suggested that Tessie sell her properties and make a nice home for them in the countryside. She refused. "I'd rather be an electric light pole on Powell Street," she said, "than own all the lands in the sticks."

Also in 1909, San Franciscans chose as their mayor a former

president of the Building Trade Council, P. H. McCarthy. His campaign slogan was "Make San Francisco the Paris of America." The manager of the "McCarthy Non-Political Liberty League" was Jerome Bassity. He, McCarthy, and Police Commissioner Harry P. Flannery (owner of the Richelieu Bar at the junction of Market, Kearny, and Geary Streets) became a ruling triumvirate.

When the grand jury that indicted Schmitz and Ruef delved into Bassity's business past, it recommended that he not be permitted to build a huge brothel on Commercial Street that would accommodate one hundred women. "I don't care a snap for the grand jury," said Bassity. "I'm going to open, and they can't stop me." He did so on December 17, 1906, with a one-night-only, no-charge policy. He remained an important underworld figure until a reform government shut down the vice trade in 1917. When the ex-king of the Barbary Coast died in San Diego on August 14, 1929, he was worth less than ten thousand dollars.

By the time the brothels, gambling dens, and saloons were being driven out of business, General Frederick Funston was no longer on duty at the Presidio. After serving in Kansas at Fort Leavenworth, he participated in a so-called Punitive Expedition against the Mexican terrorist Pancho Villa (a hero to Mexicans). For a mission to Santa Cruz, he was promoted to major general, the army's highest rank at that time. He then oversaw the federalization of 150,000 men of the National Guard in preparation for United States' entry into World War I. He had expected to be assigned to a significant post with General John J. "Black Jack" Pershing's American Expeditionary Force, but suffered a fatal heart attack on February 19, 1917. As his body lay in state at the Alamo in San Antonio, Texas, ten thousand mourners passed by his coffin to pay their respects. Taken to San Francisco, the body was on view in the rotunda of the new City Hall for two days. He was buried in full-dress uniform at the Presidio, overlooking the city he'd saved. President Woodrow Wilson wrote, "His genius and manhood brought order out of confusion, confidence out of fear, and much comfort in distress."

Funston's old friend and famed Kansas journalist, William Allen

White, saw him as "one of the most colorful figures in the American Army from the day of Washington on down." Allen wrote, "We had a man as dashing as [Phillip] Sheridan, as unique and picturesque as the slow-moving, taciturn [Ulysses S.] Grant, as charming as [Stonewall] Jackson, as witty as old Billy [William T.] Sherman, [and] as brave as [John] Paul Jones."

Had Funston lived to fight in France, he might have encountered James Hopper. A war correspondent for *Collier's*, he returned to write a book of sketches about its heroes titled *Medals of Honor*. Fashioning a reputation as an author, he became a resident and founder, along with Jack London, Sinclair Lewis, Upton Sinclair, and others, of an artists' and writers' colony on the Monterey Peninsula at Carmel-by-the-sea. He published short stories and books, primarily for children. "Few writers," said a reviewer in the *Boston Transcript*, "are so happily able to catch the spirit of childhood." As the director of the Federal Writers' Project for Northern California, he supervised and contributed to the *Guide to Death Valley* (1939). His *California: Guide to the Golden State* was published in 1942. He died in Carmel a month after his eightieth birthday.

Thirty years after the 1906 quake, a spectacular, pyramid-shaped skyscraper arose on a block of Montgomery Street where Hopper and other writers had lived. Known as the "Monkey Block," its bohemian inhabitants included Twain, Harte, Ambrose Bierce, Kathleen Morris, and George Sterling. It became home to the headquarters of the Transamerica Company, and remains today a towering emblem of modern San Francisco.

That San Francisco had risen from the rubble and ash of the earthquake and conflagration and was open for business was proclaimed in 1915 with a world's fair in the Marina District. Called the Panama-Pacific Exposition, it celebrated the opening of the Panama Canal. Eleven years later, the city celebrated the completion of the Golden Gate Bridge, then the world's longest suspension span, and a simultaneous opening of the San Francisco-Oakland Bay Bridge.

Taking note of the nationwide fanfare around the debut of the spectacular bridges and a flurry of articles in magazines and newspapers about the city's comeback from the earthquake, Hollywood provided a cinematic valentine titled *San Francisco*. Starring Clark Gable, Spencer Tracy, and the queen of movie musicals, Jeanette McDonald, it was set in the city in the days before the earthquake. It climaxed with a dramatic re-creation of the calamity. But as the film was being edited, someone noticed that some scenes shot in San Francisco contained glimpses of the Golden Gate Bridge. With the anachronistic frames excised, the movie gave Miss McDonald a song, "San Francisco, Open Your Golden Gate," which would remain the city's anthem until Tony Bennett's 1963 hit recording, "I Left My Heart in San Francisco."

A year before Gable and Tracy emoted in a silver screen city which movie audiences knew was doomed, Hollywood's diva of melodramas, Miriam Hopkins, portrayed a dance hall queen, co-starring with Edward G. Robinson, Joel McRae, and Brian Donlevy in *Barbary Coast*.

Describing the vibrant city of 1939 which supplanted that of Mayor Schmitz, Abraham Ruef, Jerome Bassity, and James Hopper, the Federal Writers' Project's guide to California noted, "Perhaps some of San Francisco's glamor has been drowned under a flood of neon lights; skyscrapers have replaced some of the rambling buildings mellowed by time and weather; and old-timers lament the happy-go-lucky days 'before the fire.' But it is still a gay city, convivial and dignified, for its gayety has always worn a silk hat; and it heatedly objects to the nickname 'Frisco,' used by unsuspecting outsiders. San Francisco has granite qualities as well; fogs cannot dampen its ardor; earthquakes, political scandals, and labor wars have failed to shake its confidence in itself and the future; it has remained unmistakably itself. It is still 'the City.' "

To formally salute its renaissance in 1939, San Francisco invited the entire world to the Golden Gate International Exposition. A west coast rival of the New York World's Fair of 1939–1940, it was built on man-made land called Treasure Island. With the closing of the exposition, the island was transformed into a terminal for a fleet of giant

Pan American Airways' "flying clipper ships," which enhanced the city's role as America's gateway to the Orient by providing passenger service across the Pacific.

Again capitalizing on the nation's interest in San Francisco, Hollywood used Treasure Island's exposition as the backdrop for a mystery, *Charlie Chan at Treasure Island.* But it was three years later, in 1942, that San Francisco became the backdrop for the movies' best detective yarn. Humphrey Bogart as private-investigator Samuel Spade tangled with mysterious fat-man Sydney Greenstreet, debonair Peter Lorre, dangerous gunman Elisha Cook, Jr., and duplicitous Mary Astor in chasing a fabulous statuette of a black bird in *The Maltese Falcon,* based on the novel by Dashiell Hammett, a former San Francisco private eye.

In 1944, Wallace Beery starred in *Barbary Coast Gent.* Eight years later, Joel McRae was back in town in *San Francisco Story*, this time with Yvonne DeCarlo, during the gold rush.

In 1954, *The Caine Mutiny* provided spectacular views of the Golden Gate Bridge as the U.S. Navy minesweeper of the title passed beneath.

San Francisco's notoriously steep hills provided thrills as Steve McQueen careened down them during a car chase in 1968's *Bullit.*

The first television program in which San Francisco was a star, *The Lineup,* with Warner Anderson and Tom Tulley, was produced in cooperation with the San Francisco Police Department and ran from 1954 to 1960. Rock Hudson was commissioner of police, married to Susan Saint James, in *McMillan and Wife* (1971 to 1977). Portraying a team of SFPD detectives, Karl Malden and Michael Douglas starred in *The Streets of San Francisco* from 1972 to 1977.

Each of these television dramas, in one way or another, reflected what was going on in the city of its time. The San Francisco of the 1950s became a center for "Beat Generation" poets, whom local columnist Herb Caen named "Beatniks." Sixties folk singers gathered in these small clubs of North Beach. The Purple Onion and other spots offered stages to iconoclastic comedians led by acerbic

Mort Sahl. Then came a "Haight-Ashbury" counter-culture of "hippies" and "flower children." Extolling "sex, drugs and rock and roll," protesting the war in Vietnam, and railing against "the establishment," they vowed never to trust anyone over the age of thirty.

Always a city known for a liberal social and cultural outlook and acceptance of people with alternative lifestyles, the city in the 1970s gained a reputation as a haven for homosexuals. By the century's end, a gay population centered in the Castro section had emerged as a political force with the power to decide elections and put friendly politicians into local and national offices, or defeat anyone they deemed their enemies.

Yet, ever in the back of the minds of San Franciscans in the decades since 1906 lurked the possibility of another major earthquake. Any day could bring "the big one" to test the durability of all that had been re-built, including the new skyscrapers with glass walls. To prepare for such an event, the city had instituted numerous regulations that required earthquake safeguards. But a portion of the city rested on the same man-made ground that had shifted disastrously in 1906. Huge amounts of rubble and debris from the 1906 quake had been used as landfill to create new building space. An engineering study sponsored by the insurance industry in 1987 warned that a major quake could be expected to start 79 fires, and that equipment and men to fight them would be insufficient, resulting in an estimated destruction of 22,500 to 48,000 buildings at a cost of two to five billion dollars. The U.S. National Oceanic and Atmospheric Administration predicted that a quake of the magnitude of 1906 (estimated at 8.3 on the Richter scale) would injure 40,000 people and kill more than ten thousand.

The quake that struck on October 19, 1989, was a magnitude 7.1. (A 5.2 aftershock struck 37 minutes later.) The worst jolt since 1906, it began just before the third game of the World Series at Candlestick Park, and collapsed part of the San Francisco-Oakland Bay Bridge. Damage was estimated at almost three billion dollars, about one-half the total damage in the entire earthquake zone.

Thrown into darkness for the first time since the 1906 quake and fire, the city would not have power fully restored for a day. A fire in the 911 emergency telephone service equipment room left the city dependent on an antiquated system of fire alarm boxes for three days. At least 27 blazes broke out across the city, including a major one in the Marina District where apartment buildings sank into a lagoon that had been filled with mud in preparation for the 1915 Panama-Pacific International Exposition. As in 1906, citizens formed bucket brigades to help fire fighters who were without water because of broken mains.

Interstate Highway 280 rocked so viciously during the quake that sections of the freeway slammed into one another and broke off. The Embarcadero Freeway along the waterfront was nearly destroyed. The former Albert Pike Memorial Building on Geary Boulevard was as badly damaged as it had been during the 1906 earthquake. On October 18, a U-2 spy plane from Beale Air Force Base flew over the city to take photos to be used to detect problems in structures. A survey by the Department of Public Works found damage to the Asian Art Museum, de Young Museum, California Palace of the Legion of Honor, Main Library, Hall of Justice, Opera House, Richmond Police Station, Candlestick Park, the airport, and Pier 45. Independent Insurance Agents of America said the earthquake was the sixth costliest disaster in history, exceeding one billion dollars in damage. But the Association of California Insurance Companies said insurance payout for earthquake damage could reach two billion dollars. Economist Frank McCormick of the Bank of America in San Francisco said it was likely to reach ten billion.

Deaths totaled 62, with 3,200 injured and 12,000 left homeless.

When Congress began debate on an earthquake relief bill, Representative Nancy Pelosi of California said, "We were hit by ten times the amount of explosive power of World War II, including the atomic bomb. Please give us a chance to rebuild." But a Wisconsin congressman complained that, with the median home price in San Francisco at $350,000, Californians did not need help because of their waste and affluence.

While one clergyman asserted that God had sent the earth-quake to punish San Francisco for its sins and for allowing gays to re-side there, the Rev. Billy Graham, in touring the Marina District, said, "I don't think we can say this earthquake was sent by God. We have to keep in mind that he is a God of love, mercy. Why this earthquake took place, I can't explain. I can only explain God gives grace, peace, and strength to those who trust in Him."

With tourism down ten to twenty percent, Mayor Art Agnos and a delegation of city leaders made a three-day cross-country jun-ket to meet with executives of the travel industry to explain recovery plans and assure them that San Francisco would soon be the same great place to visit that it had always been.

Their message was the same one that San Franciscans of the 1906 quake and fire had shouted to the nation and world, that when Jack London had pronounced that San Francisco was "gone," he was wrong.

Author's Note

HE OCCASION OF MY FIRST VISIT TO SAN Francisco was a weekend pass from the U.S. Army. The year was 1958. Although I had just earned a master's degree in journalism from the University of Iowa, I was a lowly private first class, and in the wisdom of whoever it was within the Pentagon with the job of classifying new soldiers, I was deemed qualified to learn Romanian in a nine-month course at the Army Language School. It was at the Presidio of Monterey, a hundred miles or so south of San Francisco. By some kind of miracle or Army over-sight, a buddy, also a private, had clearance to have a car on post. Four decades later, details of our drive up to San Francisco do not spring readily from my memory, but I do recall that the cheap hotel we chose was a mercifully short walk uphill from Market Street.

Remembering the movie *San Francisco* with Clark Gable and Spencer Tracy that ended with the quake of 1906, I wondered if the hotel had been built to survive a repeat. But more on my mind were the Beatniks. I'd heard much about the Beat Generation, read Jack Kerouac's novel *On the Road,* and devoured Allen Ginsberg's Beat poem, *Howl.* The latter was in print because the author had beaten a lawsuit concerning its suitability for publication on the allegation that it was out-and-out pornographic. With censorship laws out the window as a result, I'd rushed to buy a copy of *Howl* at a bookstore in Monterey.

With this background, I was eager to explore the section of the city made famous, or notorious, by the Beats. I knew the area only

189

as North Beach. My buddy and I found it, but our civilian clothes were insufficient to draw attention away from the haircuts that marked us a couple of nascent GIs and as un-Beatnik as anybody could get. Except for my brief contemplation of the Gable-Tracy movie, at no time on that weekend did my pal and I let the fact that we were in a city that had been knocked flat by the greatest earthquake in American history dampen our fun.

Six years later, I was back in San Francisco under far different circumstances. As a news writer and producer with ABC News, I was part of a radio team covering the Republican Party National Convention that nominated Arizona Senator Barry Goldwater for president. My work left no time between convention events to explore sites of the Great Quake of '06, but I did manage to make a return visit to North Beach. By then, the Beatniks had given way to the "folkies," who in turn were destined to give way to the Beatles when the latter arrived on U.S. shores. I recall that during a break in the entertainment in a folk music bistro in the South of Market area, I asked one of the folk singers, a native San Franciscan, if he ever worried about "the big one" that the geologists were predicting was long overdue. His reply was a brave little laugh intended to convey he didn't, but it was nervous enough to say he did.

When the city was struck by the quake in 1989, I watched the effects on television while preparing to leave on a government assignment to work with refugee-journalists who'd been driven out Afghanistan by the Russians to the city of Peshawar, Pakistan. Comforted that the '89 quake was not "the big one," and confident that San Francisco would be prepared for it when it came, I confined the subject to the back of my mind. Consequently, when Nick Lyon, owner of The Lyons Press, for whom I'd written a book on cigars, asked my literary agent, Jake Elwell, if he thought I might be interested in doing a book on the 1906 quake, I knew little more about it than the fictionalized version of the old Gable-Tracy movie.

To begin my research, I turned first to the Internet Web site of the San Francisco Museum and found it to be a treasure trove, not only of the facts of the calamity, but also of personal accounts of the quake and fire and contemporary newspaper and magazine articles. Suddenly, what I'd expected to be a story of general devastation became personalized, from the rather comic figure of Enrico Caruso threatened with the theft of his trunks to the heroism of Navy Lieutenant Frederick Freeman, the audacity of General Frederick Funston, scheming by Abraham Ruef, an oddly sympathetic scoundrel mayor rising to meet the crisis, the dauntless journalism of James Hopper and Jack London, and personalities in the city, state, and the federal governments struggling to cope with the worst disaster in U.S. history. All of this happened decades before routine television news reports of aid being rushed to a disaster by airplanes and the existence of the Federal Emergency Management Agency (FEMA).

Having written books about Theodore Roosevelt, I was not surprised that his pride would not permit him to accept generous offers of assistance from other governments. Neither was I at all amazed at the outpouring of aid from Americans, nor that William Randolph Hearst found an opportunity to both help the city of his birth and sell newspapers. As a lifetime journalist, I was keenly interested in the role of the coverage of the earthquake and fire by the newspapers of San Francisco and the nation. Brimming with the overall extent of the calamity, they provided vivid stories of individuals whose lives were shattered, temporarily or forever.

Available to me were numerous books that were published soon after the quake, each of which provided stories of people who had been shaken from their beds at 5:13 A.M. on April 18, 1906, yet managed to cope with the loss of loved ones, their homes, and property, and could even crack a joke or offer a stranger a spirit-bolstering song. Among such volumes were *The History of the San Francisco Disaster and Mount Vesuvius Horror,* by Charles Eugene Banks and Opie Reed, and Charles Morris's *The San Francisco Calamity by Earthquake and by Fire,* both of which were published in 1906. Especially helpful in describing the Barbary Coast and its most audacious denizen, Jerome Bassity, was Herbert Asbury's *The Barbary Coast* (1933).

Other archives on the quake and the people it affected are maintained by the California Historical Society, San Francisco; Bancroft Library, University of California at Berkeley; the San Francisco Historical Society, San Francisco History Association, San Francisco Public Library; United States Geological Survey, Menlo Park, California; Chinatown Library, San Francisco; de Young Museum, San Francisco; and California State Archives, the California State Library, and the California Military Museum, Sacramento. The life and Army career of General Funston have been memorialized at the Allen County Historical Society and the Funston Boyhood Home, Iola, Kansas; and the Museum of the Kansas National Guard, Topeka, Kansas.

Especially enlightening in providing an overview of the quake and fire as I began my work were two splendid recent books, *Denial of Disaster: The Untold Story and Photographs of the San Francisco Earthquake and Fire of 1906,* by Gladys Hansen and Emmett Condon, and Dan Kurzman's *Disaster! The Great San Francisco Earthquake and Fire of 1906.*

Insights into the history, geography, architecture, culture, commerce, and life in general, in San Francisco before April 18, 1906, were found in *Baedeker's United States 1893,* along with biographies of Mark Twain and Bret Harte. A portrait of the city 33 years later was provided by the *WPA Guide to California,* produced by the Federal Writers' Project.

In researching San Francisco, I came across numerous quotations on the subject of its lasting allure. Since the anonymous pioneer who first called the link between the Pacific Ocean and a beautiful bay "the golden gate," describing San Francisco has challenged everyone who sets foot there. William Howard Taft called it "the city that knows how." To journalist, poet, novelist, and San Francisco resident Ambrose Bierce it was mythical.

"San Francisco has only one drawback," said Rudyard Kipling. "'Tis hard to leave."

Mark Twain declared, "I have always been rather better treated in San Francisco than I actually deserved." For author and playwright

William Saroyan, San Francisco was itself art, and above all literary art. "Every block is a short story, every hill a novel," he wrote. "Every home a poem, every dweller within immortal. This is the whole truth."

Jazz composer and musician Duke Ellington said, "San Francisco is one of the great cultural plateaus of the world." On his 50th birthday, native San Franciscan Joe Dimaggio said, "I'm proud to have been a [New York] Yankee. But I have found more happiness and contentment since I came back home to San Francisco than any man has a right to deserve. This is the friendliest city in the world." Visiting Russian President Mikhail Gorbachev told a group of San Francisco officials, "You are fortune to live here. If I were your president I would levy a tax on you for living in San Francisco."

Before venturing to the city by the bay during a lecture tour across the United States in 1882, Irish playwright Oscar Wilde told a group of friends, "It's an odd thing, but anyone who disappears is said to have been seen in San Francisco. It must be a delightful city and possess all the attractions of the next world."

After visiting the San Francisco Bohemian Club, Wilde quipped, "I never saw so many well-dressed, well-fed, business-looking Bohemians in my life."

Evangelist Billy Graham declared, "The Bay Area is so beautiful, I hesitate to preach about heaven while I'm here."

Speculating on the possibility of one day finding himself standing before Saint Peter at the pearly gates of paradise, popular San Francisco newspaper columnist Herb Caen put it best. He said, "I'll look around and say, 'It ain't bad, but it ain't San Francisco.' "

Further Reading

Aitken, Frank. *A History of the Earthquake and Fire.* San Francisco: E. Hilton, 1906.

Asbury, Herbert. *The Barbary Coast.* New York: Capricorn, 1933.

Banks, Charles Eugene, and Opie Read. *The History of the San Francisco Disaster and Mount Vesuvius Horror.* San Francisco: C. E. Thomas, 1906.

Barker, Malcolm E., compiled and introduction by. *Three Fearful Days: San Francisco Memoirs of the 1906 Earthquake and Fire.* San Francisco: Londonborn Publications, 1998.

Bean, Walton. *Boss Ruef's San Francisco.* London: Cambridge University Press, 1952.

Bronson, William. *The Earth Shook, the Sky Burned.* New York: Doubleday, 1959.

Brown, Helen Hillyer. *The Great San Francisco Fire.* San Francisco: Leo Holub, 1956.

Dickelmann, William. *San Francisco Earthquake Fire, April 18, 1906.* San Francisco, 1906.

Dolan, Edward F. *Disaster 1906: The San Francisco Earthquake and Fire.* New York: Julius Messner, 1967.

Greely, Adolphus. *Earthquake in California, April 18, 1906.* Washington, D.C.: U.S. Government Printing Office, 1906.

Hansen, Gladys, and Emmett Condon. *Denial of Disaster: The Untold Story and Photographs of the San Francisco Earthquake and Fire of 1906.* San Francisco: Cameron and Company, 1989.

Jordan, David S. *The California Earthquake of 1906*. San Francisco: Robertson, 1907.

Keeler, Charles. *San Francisco Through Earthquake and Fire*. San Francisco: Paul Elder, 1906.

Kennedy, John Castillo. *The Great Earthquake and Fire, San Francisco, 1906*. New York: William Morrow, 1963.

Kurzman, Dan. *Disaster! The Great San Francisco Earthquake and Fire of 1906*. New York: William Morrow, 2001.

Linthicum, R., and T. White. *The Complete Story of the San Francisco Horror*. Chicago: Herbert Russell, 1906.

Mack, Gerstle. *1906: Surviving the Great Earthquake and Fire*. San Francisco: Chronicle Books, 1981.

Pan, Erica Y. Z. *The Impact of the 1906 Earthquake on San Francisco's Chinatown*. New York: Peter Lang, 1995.

Searight, Frank. *The Doomed City*. Chicago: Laird & Lee, 1906.

Sutherland, Monica. *The Damndest Finest Ruins*. New York: Coward-McCann, 1959.

Thomas, Gordon, and Max Morgan. *The San Francisco Earthquake*. New York: Stein and Day, 1971.

Wilson, James Russell. *San Francisco's Horror of Earthquake and Fire*. San Francisco: Memorial Publishing Company, 1906.

Index